Wicked
SYRACUSE

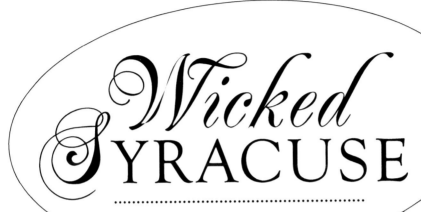

Wicked SYRACUSE

Neil K. MacMillan

A History of Sin in Salt City

THE
History
PRESS

Published by The History Press
Charleston, SC 29403
www.historypress.net

First published 2013

Manufactured in the United States

ISBN 978.1.60949.752.1

Library of Congress CIP data applied for.

CONTENTS

Acknowledgements   7
Introduction   9

1. Ringing in the New Year: The Cook Coffee House Riot   13
2. Fanning the Flames: Three Notable Arson Cases   17
3. The Dashing Train Robber   21
4. Broken Chains   25
5. Soiled Doves and Sporting Houses   31
6. Making Money the Old-fashioned Way   34
7. "Bud" and "Momsie"   38
8. Fallen Heroes: Detective Harvey, Patrolman Near,
   Patrolman Hannon and Officer Jarmacz   41
9. Toddy Stricken: Demon Rum and Prohibition   45
10. Bad Trips: Illegal Drugs in the City   50
11. "That's Where the Money Is": Bank Robbery   54
12. The Weird and Unusual: Crimes of the Heart   57
13. Ransom and Ruin: Kidnapping   61
14. Making Money the Old-fashioned Way II: Counterfeiting
    and Forgery   64
15. Murder Most Foul   68
16. The Weird and Unusual: Some People Will Steal Anything   72
17. "Can't We All Just Get Along?": Assault   76
18. Criminal Combines: Gangs in Syracuse   79

CONTENTS

19. Making Money the Old-fashioned Way III: Schemes,
    Frauds and Con Games   84
20. Vandalism for Fun and Maybe Profit   87
21. No Joy in This Ride: Vehicle Theft   91
22. Roll Them Bones: Gambling in the Salt City   95
23. Hell No, I Won't Go: Draft Dodgers and Bounty Jumpers   99
24. Rape   101
25. The Weird and Unusual: "You Stole What?"   105
26. Civil Unrest: Other Riots in the Salt City   109
27. Making Money the Old-fashioned Way IV: More Frauds
    and Schemes   113
28. The Weird and Unusual: More Crimes of the Heart   117
29. Getting Horizontal: More Prostitution in Syracuse   120
30. Smut Happens: Obscenity Cases in Syracuse   125
31. Speak Softly and Carry a Big Stick: The Roosevelt/Barnes Trial 129
32. Syracuse and Crime: A Comparison of Then and Now   133

Epilogue   137
Notes   139
About the Author   141

ACKNOWLEDGEMENTS

I'd like to acknowledge the staff at the Onondaga Historical Association for the incalculable assistance they tendered me throughout this project. The *Post-Standard* Newspaper Archives proved an invaluable resource at every step and turn. Thanks to the staff at The History Press for their guidance, especially my commissioning editor, Whitney Tarella Landis. Thanks are also due to the many friends and relations who offered hints and rumors to follow up on and lastly but always first in my heart, my wife, Peggy. I dedicate this work to those who fostered my love of history: my father, Vernon MacMillan; my mother, Betty Stanton MacMillan; Mrs. Florence Supnik, teacher, mentor and historian; Lawrence Grant Allen, soldier, scholar, mentor and friend; and Professors Mary Borden, Deb Holler, Yvonne Murphy and Mark Soderstrom of SUNY Empire State College for giving me the tools to adequately express my love of history.

INTRODUCTION

Walk with me. You don't need a jacket. We're not going far. We all hear the history of our families, our homes, our country, but we don't often hear the whole story. Some things hide in the dark. We're going to peek in the shadows where the often-untold stories lurk.

Like any city, Syracuse holds secrets. Some secrets are simply things that don't get said, but others are juicy—the stuff scandals, soap operas and miniseries are made of. If stalwart heroes made Syracuse a vibrant, growing city, so too did the miscreants that dot the city's history.

Let's face it—good and evil co-exist, and we all love a scandalous story. If we need examples like Ephraim Webster and James Geddes to uphold as paragons of the pioneer spirit and work ethic, we also need the examples of Oliver Curtis Perry, Benjamin Roscoe and Zachariah Freeman for moral comparison. French philosopher Georges Santayana said, "Those who ignore history are condemned to repeat it." We learn from our mistakes—or we're supposed to, anyway.

Syracuse was and is a city built by immigration. To be sure, a fair portion of the population came from New England stock, but from the earliest days, immigrants played an ever-growing part in the city's history. All facets of life in Syracuse were affected and continue to be by immigrants. Yet it would be too easy and quite erroneous to label crime then—as now—as an immigrant problem. Syracuse and the United States both have a rich criminal history.

As Syracuse grew, so too did the criminal elements. In the period between 1840 and 1890, when the electric chair was used for the first time, only

Syracuse in 1855 was a thriving town, thanks to the salt industry and the Erie Canal. But with prosperity came crime. *Courtesy of the Library of Congress.*

four people were hanged in Onondaga County. The first was the above-mentioned Mr. Freeman. Salt built Syracuse, and salt boilers would prove to be some of the first criminals in the city. With the Erie Canal came criminals

from other areas following the water way colloquially known as "Clinton's Ditch" seeking to ply their nefarious trades. From a sleepy village originally known as Bogardus Corners, Syracuse grew to a city of over 100,000 people. There were killings, and there were rescues of African Americans who fled to Syracuse in search of freedom only to be confronted with the cruelty of the Fugitive Slave Act. There were thieves and con artists, some of them under the guise of official duty. There were violators of the Volstead Act, which outlawed the sale of alcohol, and there were, how shall we put this delicately, practitioners of the world's oldest profession.

I chose to focus on the period before 1950 for several reasons. I am a historian with a focus on the mid-nineteenth century, and so there is a natural gravitation to that time period. Secondly, there is an old adage: the more things change, the more they stay the same. If you name a crime we have now, it's certain that our ancestors dealt with it then. Some of you will mention Internet fraud—the fraud just got faster. Third, like it or not, criminals are human. They are people like us. We are all subject to the temptation of something for nothing or the anger that urges us to do harm to someone who has wronged us. The difference, quite simply, is that most of us don't act on those impulses. Lastly, our ancestors tended to have a more cosmopolitan outlook about certain crimes. There was only white-collar crime if you got caught. They might have covered table and chair legs out of exaggerated modesty, but fraud and embezzlement were business as usual until someone got caught with their hand in the till. The hack drivers all knew where the houses of ill fame were, and so did the pillars of the community.

Shall we go? There is a chill in the air—or maybe that is the anticipation of skullduggery. What was that noise? Careful now! The alleys are dark, and mischief is afoot.

Chapter 1

RINGING IN THE NEW YEAR:
THE COOK COFFEE HOUSE RIOT

I t is a pivotal event in the history of Syracuse, and yet it is an event little known to the general populous. New Year's Day 1844 was a day of celebration for Syracuse and neighboring Salina. It was also the day that Cook's Coffee House would become rooted in the lore of Syracuse. The coffeehouse was located on the corner of Washington and South Warren Streets. The business was run by Charles Seigle and his wife, and there were plans for a dinner and dance the night of New Year's Day 1844. The coffeehouse was considered upscale and catered to Syracuse's German population. The furnishings were ornate, including much glasswork. The establishment boasted a salty old parrot well versed in tavern talk and able to recite the drinks the coffeehouse served in both German and English.

By 1844, Syracuse was a growing village and competed with the neighboring town of Salina for economic prosperity. If Syracuse had the Erie Canal, Salina, also known as Salt Point, had access to the Onondaga salt deposits. Culling salt from the deposits was backbreaking work for the men known as salt boilers. They were men who endured harsh working conditions and viewed fighting as a recreational pursuit. Most of the Salt Point boilers were Irish immigrants, and ethnic and economic rivalry lay just under the surface as the villages of Syracuse and Salina grew. Like any future conflagration, all that was needed was a good spark.

William Blake and his fellow Irish salt boilers were looking for a fight. They entered Seigle's establishment and positioned themselves throughout the large room decorated for the New Year's celebration. As in previous brawls, the Salt Pointers established a signal to start the fracas. Blake and company lubricated themselves with copious amounts of liquor for the task ahead. Draining his drink, William Blake smashed the glass on the bar.

Mrs. Seigle, the stouthearted wife of Charles, was not a woman to cower at a drunken display. She immediately confronted Blake. Harsh words were traded, and Blake insulted Mrs. Seigle. The German hausfrau may have slapped the salt boiler, because then, all hell broke loose! Calling for aid, Mrs. Seigle summoned her husband, who fired a load of buckshot at Blake. It was rumored at the time that Charles Seigle knew the fight was imminent. The loaded shotgun[1] may have been a prudent precaution. More shots were fired, and someone ran for the sheriff.

The sheriff was conscientious and courageous, but the fight escalated into a riot, and he was out of his league. Several shots peppered the tavern, and the riot showed no signs of abating. Infuriated curses in German and English spilled from the coffeehouse. Amid the carnage, the salty old parrot hurled its own epithets at all participants as Charles Seigle retreated to hide in a closet.

Captain Timothy Teall's Syracuse Cadets Militia was ready to return to their homes that Monday evening when word of the riot reached them. Lieutenant William B. Olmstead was not a man to shirk in his duty. Calling the unit back, he formed them up and marched them to the coffeehouse. He ordered the militia to load and fix bayonets. The rioters dispersed but returned to clear out the coffeehouse furniture, burning it in a bonfire. Someone also stole $300 from the Seigles. The militia returned, and several of the rioters were arrested.

Charles Seigle disappeared but was taken into custody a couple of days later. The court determined that he had acted in defense of his wife and property, and he was released. Though it was believed William Blake's injuries were fatal, the salt boiler lived. The riot, an ugly little incident in the history of Syracuse, fueled by drink and ethnic bigotry, compelled the proponents of merging the village of Syracuse with portions of Salina and led to the incorporation of the City of Syracuse in 1848.

Like the era of the salt boiler, Cook's Coffee House is long gone. In April 1844, after several death threats, Charles Seigle sold the business to Eliphalet Welch and moved to Milwaukee with his wife. In 1867, the building was moved to the corner of Montgomery and Jackson Streets to make way for the Vanderbilt House, an upscale hotel. The building no longer stands.

Key Bank stands where Cook's Coffee House once stood. The tavern owned by Charles Seigle was the site of the notorious riot. *Courtesy of Neil K. MacMillan.*

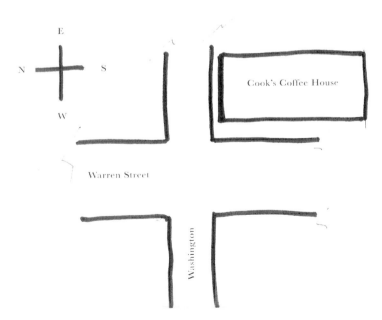

Map (not to scale) showing the location of Cook's Coffee House in 1844. It is now the site of the First Trust Bank building. *Courtesy of Neil K. MacMillan.*

It fell to the wrecking ball in the 1950s when the area underwent major urban renewal. The Vanderbilt has since been replaced by the First Trust Bank building. The riot also led to a better-equipped sheriff's department and a police department for the city of Syracuse. The previous town line is remembered in Division Street on the city's north side. The New Year's celebration that went horribly wrong helped to catapult Syracuse into a major city in New York State.

Chapter 2

FANNING THE FLAMES:
THREE NOTABLE ARSON CASES

Fire has served man in a variety of ways, both beneficial and nefarious. But like any tool, fire can be misused. In some cases, kids playing with matches or people falling asleep with a cigarette burning led to the inferno. In others, the fire is intentionally set.

Like most cities, Syracuse has had its share of arson cases, and indeed the crime continues to plague Syracuse and the nation. Three cases stand out in Syracuse's history, all of them with tragic overtones. In two of the cases, fraud seemed to be the overriding motive. In the third, mental illness played a part.

December 26, 1869, should have been a time of joy and quietude. Instead, it would be remembered as the start of one of Syracuse's most notorious fraud and arson cases. Simply put, money motivated all the participants. In a bid to collect on an insurance policy issued to Samuel Bennett, William Craig's house was set ablaze. Four men were charged in connection with the fire that damaged William H. Craig's domicile and the belongings of Samuel F. Bennett.

F.P. Vedder, Samuel F. Bennett, Edward F. Briggs and Adam Fralick were all charged with arson. Bail for the first three men was set at $20,000, while Fralick's was set at $30,000 because he had actually set the fire. These were enormous amounts in an era in which the average policeman made $1,200 a year and a private in the army made just $13 a month. Two other men, Noah B. Broughton and Dr. Abram Babcock, were indicted for obstruction of justice when they tried to have Mr. Vedder ensconced in an insane asylum for the purposes of avoiding prosecution. Vedder confessed to being commissioned by Bennett to purchase bonds after the fire and to discussing the fire after the fact.

Samuel Bennett opted for a separate trial. The proceedings lasted almost three years. Adam Fralick was found guilty of arson in the first degree and sentenced to a term in Auburn Prison. He had agreed to buy goods from Bennett that were later listed as destroyed in the fire. He committed suicide by overdosing on morphine, maintaining his innocence to the end. The insurance companies were successful in their lawsuit to recover all monies paid to Bennett and his co-conspirators.

James Bradt was a dentist whose life was about to take a dramatic turn for the worse in the month of July 1875, when on July 20, fire broke out in the Kirk Block. James Parks discovered the fire and woke his neighbor, Dr. Bradt. Both men escaped the fire, and no one was injured. After the fire was extinguished, police combed through the damaged building and found a demijohn[2] of kerosene and a sprinkling can. There was also a trail of kerosene from Dr. Bradt's door to Mr. Fowler's door and an auger hole and wood shards. Fowler was another tenant of the building. Officers Charles Doolittle and Prettie quickly took the dentist into custody.

Coming almost on the heels of the Bennett case, the trial of Dr. Bradt was a dream come true for the journalists of the day. Though there was evidence that arson had been committed, Dr. Bradt was acquitted. When looking at this case, there are several things that struck me. Foremost among these is the fact that no one else was indicted for the arson. It is easy to look back at the Kirk Block fire and think, "Today, we would have the evidence and scientific knowledge to convict Bradt or find the real culprit." Perhaps. However, in 1875, there was no such thing as fingerprint evidence—let alone DNA—and even today we send innocent people to prison because of human error. The court found Dr. Bradt innocent. Unless additional evidence is uncovered to shed light on this murky crime, only the arsonist will know the truth, and he isn't speaking.

Mystery comes in many forms. How do we explain the workings of the Crandall arson? Among the enigmas in the case is Mr. Crandall himself. His name was alternately listed as Horace J. Crandall, Homer N. Crandall, Homer J. Crandall and H.J. Crandall. Equally murky were Mr. Crandall's motives.

Opposite, bottom: This New York Fire Department fire engine would have been a common sight on Syracuse streets in 1910, and that had not changed much in the thirty-one years between the Crandall fire and when this picture was taken. *Courtesy of the Library of Congress.*

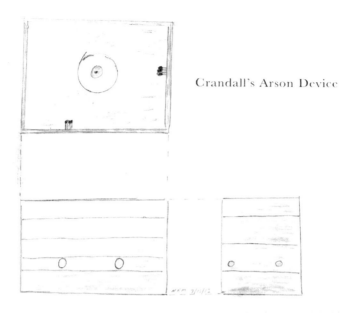

Crandall's Arson Device

A drawing of one of the arson boxes used by Homer Crandall. The drawing is based on newspaper accounts of the arson investigation. *Courtesy of Neil K. MacMillan.*

The evening of Wednesday, July 30, 1879, was promising to be nothing unusual for Mrs. Augusta Hall as she went about her duties at 312 Mulberry Street in the village of Danforth. The village, now part of the city of Syracuse, was an upscale neighborhood. Mrs. Hall worked for the Crandall family, who was out visiting for the evening as the servant made her way through her tasks. Seeing a light in the basement, Augusta went to investigate. What she discovered changed her life dramatically.

It was an ingenious device. A pine box showed the light of a candle in another pine box filled with cotton, paper, rosin, matches and other flammable objects working as a timed incendiary device. The police were called, and in their investigation discovered a second box in the barn. The arsonist had designed the infernal device to be fired remotely. It featured a bundle of matches able to be drawn against a length of sand paper with a string from the house, enabling them to strike and ignite the flammables in the second box.[3] A latticework grill made of painted wood connected the Crandall barn and house. Augusta Hall was quickly placed under arrest.

Mrs. Hall was quickly exonerated, and suspicion fell on Homer Crandall. What made Crandall decide to burn his own house? We may never know save the catchall phrase of mental instability. There was a touch of genius— evil genius, to be sure, but genius nonetheless. Homer was quickly arrested, and bail was set at $6,000, a substantial sum in the Gilded Age. It was rumored that Crandall had confessed, but that was strictly rumor. Homer Crandall was examined by doctors and removed to the State Asylum for the Insane for a year.

Arson continues to plague Syracuse, though not with such widespread revulsion and fascination as it did in the three cases above.

Chapter 3

THE DASHING TRAIN ROBBER

When we think of train robbery, we conjure up images of the Old West and Frank and Jesse James or Butch Cassidy and the Sundance Kid. Saturday morning television shaped the minds of many children of my generation about the Wild West and train robbers. Who among us didn't play cops and robbers growing up? Our ideas were romanticized tripe painting bank and train robbers as heroes unjustly set upon by an unfeeling and oppressive government bought and sold by the railroads and banks. The names are legendary, but one name is curiously absent from the roster.

Oliver Curtis Perry was born in 1864 in a New York City tenement. He claimed to be related to Oliver Hazard Perry, the naval hero of the War of 1812. The story, like others of Perry's, should be taken with a grain of salt, but the dashing train robber certainly shared his alleged relative's bravery and élan. Perry had minimal education, as criminal historian Jay Robert Nash quotes Perry in his tome *Bloodletters and Badmen*: "I was only a lad without schooling, so I had to take bold strokes with big chances." As a young man, Perry traveled to Wyoming and worked as a cowboy. He stated that he had robbed several coaches and trains out west, although there is no verification of that. It is entirely possible that he did, but in a land of vast expanse, it is possible it was attributed to others. It is also possible that he was a fringe member of a gang and never received recognition under his own name or any of his known aliases. Of course, it is also possible that Perry made up the robberies out of whole cloth. But if he did fabricate his western criminal

Daring train robber Oliver Curtis Perry. *Courtesy of the Library of Congress.*

career, he would cement his bona fides with a rarely seen bravery and élan upon his return to New York.

Perry returned to New York in 1891. He was twenty-seven years old, tall, slender and roguishly handsome. He quickly took one of the aforementioned "bold strokes" by robbing a New York Central train near Albany on September 29. Unlike those masters of the genre the James brothers, Oliver Curtis Perry had no gang with him. Perry was the first person to rob a train solo. Cutting a hole in the baggage car, he overpowered the guards and made off with several thousand dollars in cash and jewels. Holding on with one hand, he sawed through the train's brake line and made his escape.

He next robbed a New York Central train near Syracuse, garnering a small amount for his trouble. It was February 1892, and again Perry made a quick escape. He repaired to Syracuse and lived extravagantly. The handsome robber was not averse to the ladies, nor were they to him. But living the high life proved expensive, and by September 20, 1892, Perry again needed money.

History and fortune sometimes turn on insignificant decisions. If President Lincoln had listened to his secretary and not gone to the theater, John Wilkes Booth might be nothing more than a footnote in American theater history. So, too, would Oliver Curtis Perry's decision to rob the westbound New York Central train that Tuesday. Following his usual procedure, Perry bought a ticket on the train. During his attempt to rob the train, he fought a wild fight with the guard. Perry attempted to figure out the combination to the express safe.

The unconscious guard had pulled the signal rope during the brawl with Perry. The conductor came at the double quick, and Perry threw open the door to the baggage car, diving out near the town of Jordan, New York.

Authorities had been notified of the robbery by the time the train arrived in Lyons, New York. Taking an eastbound train to Jordan, Perry was spotted by the conductor of the almost-robbed train while calmly waiting for another train. The alarm was raised, and lawmen took up the chase. Perry frantically made his way across the rail yard and found a locomotive with a full head of steam. The chase was on! In a seesaw race that could have proved

Two trains ready to steam ahead. *Courtesy of the Library of Congress.*

catastrophic, Perry tried to outrun the authorities. As the two engines traversed the rails back and forth, several shots were exchanged. It was a stalemate that Perry knew he couldn't win. Stopping the locomotive, Perry dashed for cover with the posse of lawmen hot on his heels. As the lawmen prepared to battle with Perry in a nearby swamp, Wayne County sheriff Jerry Collins asked the train robber if he wanted to fight it out. Perry declined. He was out of bullets.

It was a chase that could have inspired countless dime novels and Hollywood westerns. It was also the end of Perry's career as a train robber, as he was quickly tried, convicted and sentenced to forty-nine years in Auburn Prison. Incarceration didn't sit well with Perry, who became involved in several disturbances and was transferred to the State Hospital for the Criminally Insane at Mattawan. The guard force at the hospital was underpaid and less than vigilant in their duties, and on April 10, 1895, a female admirer sent

A locomotive similar to the one Oliver Curtis Perry commandeered in his last train robbery attempt. *Courtesy of the Library of Congress.*

Perry a Bible with a saw secreted among the pages. The Bible proved to be liberating for the outlaw.

Broke and hungry, Perry made his way to Weehawken, New Jersey, where he was captured by a town constable as he roasted a rabbit he had killed with a rock. He was then remanded to the maximum-security prison at Dannemora, New York. He was placed in solitary confinement after several abortive escape attempts.

If Perry wasn't insane when he went into Mattawan, he was certainly disturbed by his enforced solitude. In 1899, he blinded himself with a device of his own design consisting of a weighted block of wood studded with two nails. Jay Robert Nash relates that Perry told a friend in a dictated letter: "I was born in the light of day against my will, of course. I now assert my right to shut out the light." Perry passed away on September 10, 1930, ten days shy of the thirty-eighth anniversary of his failed train robbery.

Was Perry insane, or was he one of the last of a vanishing breed of desperadoes who took bold chances to make a name and a purse for themselves? Perhaps a bit of both, but in the waning years of the nineteenth century, he kept Syracuse enthralled with his exploits. I think he would be pleased that there is a following for his exploits even to this day.

Chapter 4

BROKEN CHAINS

The period between the end of the Mexican War and the start of the Civil War was a turbulent era for the United States, and Syracuse was no exception. Arguments raged in Congress, through the press and on the streets about slavery. The Compromise of 1850, in addition to modifying how slavery was treated in the territories acquired by the Mexican War, also stiffened the Fugitive Slave Law. Federal law required citizens to turn over slaves to anyone claiming them as such. Legally, this did not apply to freedmen. New York State abolished slavery in 1827. In practice, however, slave hunters could claim that any African American was a slave and require that they be seized and turned over to them. Needless to say, in Onondaga County and Syracuse, described by one Southern commentator as a "hotbed of abolitionism," the law was not popular. Men like Gerrit Smith argued that slavery was morally damaging and unconstitutional. Even the famous statesman Daniel Webster got involved in the conflict, arguing that failure to uphold the Fugitive Slave Law amounted to treason. That the Fugitive Slave Act was law was indisputable. It is equally undeniable that it wrought tragedy on a direct and personal level throughout the period of its enforcement. Families were separated, lives were ruined and people died as a result of the act.

In the early 1850s, William and Caroline Harris were traveling on a packet boat with their child. Caroline was a free mulatto, and William may have been a slave. Harwell Webster, Silas Cowell and a boatman named Cluney accosted the couple on the canal boat and threatened to turn them over to

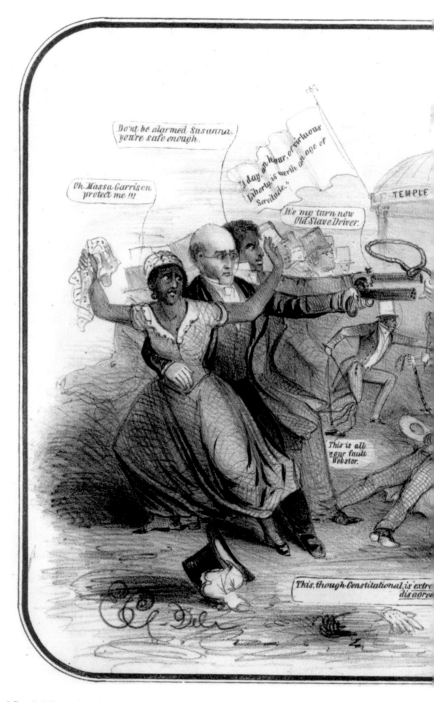

A Practical Illustration of the Fugitive Slave Law. This 1851 lithograph, a political cartoon, records the divisiveness of the act. The artist was an abolitionist, but his name is lost to us. *Courtesy of the Library of Congress.*

Syracuse authorities as runaway slaves. Caroline jumped in the canal with her three-year-old. She was saved, but the child drowned. The three men responsible for the incident were taken into custody and charged with kidnapping. The situation seems pretty straightforward today. In point of fact, it was a rarity for African Americans to receive a favorable outcome in legal disputes with whites. Coming on the heels of the strengthening of the Fugitive Slave Act, a law not viewed favorably in Syracuse, and the fact that William and Caroline suffered the loss of their child, the courts made an example of Webster, Cowell and Cluney. But it wasn't much of one. The trio was fined and sent on their way, small consolation for the parents of a murdered child.

If you've ever driven in downtown Syracuse at all, you've seen Clinton Square. On the west end of the square is a statue depicting the Jerry rescue. Unlike the Harris case, the Jerry rescue is well known and immortalized in the brick-and-stone monument. William Henry, a former slave turned barrel maker, knew the horrors of bondage. Known to his master simply as Jerry, Henry thought he was home free when he arrived in Syracuse. However, the Fugitive Slave Act brought new impetus to law enforcement and to slave owners and patrollers from the South to seize African Americans and return them to slavery. All that was required was a white man's word. It mattered little that New York was not a slave state or that Syracuse was regarded as anti-slavery. There were people ready to turn in a slave for whatever reward might be posted. William Henry also knew that it mattered little that he was a productive citizen of Syracuse.

October 1, 1851, proved a pivotal day for William Henry and Syracuse's abolitionist community, as Jerry was arrested and held by federal marshals under the provisions of the Fugitive Slave Act. William Henry would be a symbol of the government's intent to enforce the law in the North as well as the South. Word spread quickly through Syracuse's abolitionist community. Action had to be taken. As Jerry's trial moved forward, the plotters quickly assembled. It was imperative to people like Gerrit Smith and Jermain Loguen that Jerry not be returned to slavery.

Several hundred people gathered outside the Townsend Block, where federal commissioner William Sabine had his office. The building was located on the south side of Clinton Square on the corner of Clinton and Water Streets. Several of the rescuers blackened their faces much in the style of the Boston Tea Party participants. While most of the rescuers could face prison and fines, Jermain Loguen faced the prospect of being returned to slavery himself. Like William Henry, Loguen was a runaway

The Jerry Rescue monument, Clinton Square, Syracuse, New York. *Courtesy of Neil K. MacMillan.*

slave. That would have deterred many men, but Loguen was made of sterner stuff. The man who refused to purchase his freedom because it would legitimize slavery to do so never hesitated to help another slave seeking to avoid being sent south.

With little doubt that Commissioner Sabine would rule in favor of Jerry's master, the crowd stormed the Townsend Block and liberated Jerry from his jail cell. William Henry was hidden in Syracuse for a few days and then spirited to Canada via Mexico, New York and the port of Oswego on Lake Ontario. Loguen and several others also fled to Canada to avoid prosecution. Loguen eventually returned to Syracuse and remained heavily involved in bettering the lot of African Americans. Missouri-born Henry ended his days in Canada, dying in the late 1850s. The Fugitive Slave Act lasted on paper until 1864. Effective enforcement ended in 1861 with the shots fired on Fort Sumter. Noted politician and Civil War general Benjamin Butler sounded the death knell for the Fugitive Slave Act when he told a Virginia planter he could not expect a law of the United States to be enforced in a foreign country, which Virginia claimed to be at that point. The Emancipation

View of the Erie Canal looking toward Salina Street, circa 1900. The building at the right stands where the Townsend block once stood. *Courtesy of the Library of Congress.*

Proclamation and the ratification of the Thirteenth Amendment buried the Fugitive Slave Act for good.

Where are the crimes in these two cases other than the violations of the Fugitive Slave Act? If we bear in mind that we cannot do justice by applying twenty-first-century mores to two mid-nineteenth-century cases, we come up with a laundry list of violations of law extant in the early 1850s: intimidation, murder in the commission of a felony, kidnapping, assault, jail breaking, obstruction of a federal official in the course of his duties and rioting.

The Townsend Block is gone. After the rescue, it was known as the Jerry Rescue Building, though the name was never officially changed. When the Townsend Block burned, the site was colloquially still referred to as the Jerry Rescue Building. The Jerry Rescue Monument, erected in 1990, commemorates the event in which men of good character came together to defy a law they believed was morally reprehensible and liberate one man.

Chapter 5

SOILED DOVES AND SPORTING HOUSES

O ver the years, several areas in Syracuse have been notorious hot spots for prostitution. Let's face it—prostitution isn't called the oldest profession for nothing. Like any city, Syracuse has its fair share of vice. When salt and the canal made Syracuse a thriving city instead of a sleepy village, the men piloting the canal boats, boiling the salt and building the city were not averse to various forms of recreation that were not necessarily socially acceptable. Drinking, fighting, gambling and what was known during the Civil War as "horizontal refreshment" were means of blowing off steam.

Then as now, hookers[4] went where the money was, and in the heyday of the Erie Canal, that was the area not far from Clinton Square. The location served as a staging area for canal boats, and while trolling for customers in the area of Syracuse's jail and federal commissioner's office might not have been prudent, the boatmen all knew the area west of Clinton Square was known as the place to go if you were looking for love in all the wrong places. Women like Phebie[5] Empie had no compulsions about making money with the assets bestowed upon her.

We often think of the Victorian Age as one of stern-faced prudery and excessive modesty, and in some respects, it was. The outhouse, a common feature of life in the 1850s, was then referred to as the "necessary." Furniture thought to be of a feminine nature had the legs hidden with a curtain to ensure proper modesty, and certain subjects were not mentioned in polite society. This led to a myriad of euphemisms. In an era when women cloistered themselves upon suspecting pregnancy, prostitution was not referred to by that term. So, in July 1850, Phebie was charged with keeping a house of ill fame. But she was not alone. Sisters Hannah and Esther TenEyck, Sarah Marshall and Johanna Sullivan were charged along with her. At the time, city law provided for a three-month jail term in the county prison and a fine of $100.00 and an additional $50.00 a day for each day after the first conviction for keeping a house of ill fame. The wages of sin must have been pretty good in the 1850s. All of this in an era when a general in the army made between $209.50 and $720.00 a month!

As Syracuse grew and changed, so too did the areas noted for prostitution. Over the years, various areas in the city were noted as centers of prostitution, among them Warren Street and Columbus Circle near the current Onondaga County Courthouse. Since the early days of the city, vice has remained a problem in Syracuse. Indeed, on April 10, 1934, Mayor Rolland B. Marvin sent a scathing letter to Police Chief Martin L. Cadin ordering him to clean up the city and complaining that houses of prostitution were openly advertising their wares and that women were walking the streets accosting gentlemen for immoral purposes. Marvin's political opponents were accusing him of openly condoning vice, and a statement had to be made. Similar allegations crept up five years later during William Rapp's tenure as chief of police.

Another facet of prostitution was the fact that even if people were ambivalent about it, they didn't want bordellos in their neighborhoods. In fact, in 1938, anti-vice crusader Tracey Jones advocated setting up a red-light district away from residential areas if the police were not going to enforce the laws against prostitution. This was, after all, before the era when women police officers dressed as decoy prostitutes targeting "johns" and subsequently publishing their names in the newspapers for all to see. By 1949, women who lived in "disorderly houses" such as that of Ruby Lee Hinani were being charged with residing in a bordello. The term, a late 1940s euphemism for a whorehouse, was widely used by the *Syracuse Post-Standard* and other newspapers to avoid censorship problems. Ruby had also been charged with prostitution but that count was dropped.

One hundred years after Phebie Empie's brush with the law, three women were arrested for practicing the world's oldest profession. Lillian Johnson of Washington Street was arrested August 31, 1950, and served two thirty-day sentences for two counts of prostitution. Louanna Schuster, residing at the same address as Ms. Johnson, was charged with two counts of running a disorderly house and fined $250. Ruby Larkin was also arrested in the same raid and was awarded thirty days in the county penitentiary with Ms.

Johnson. The Bible says that the wages of sin is death, but in this case, it was a month in the slammer.

Prostitution has been around since the earliest days of civilization, and I seriously doubt it will disappear any time soon. Different cultures and even the same culture in different times have viewed the oldest profession in a variety of ways. Although tacitly allowed on occasion in Syracuse's history, prostitution was never openly accepted. Legislation has never truly eradicated the problem of sex for money, and legalizing it has not addressed all the accompanying and causal social ills. Until it does, there will continue to be women like Phebie Empie on the streets of Syracuse. The ills that face prostitutes today were common in the Victorian era as well. Police arrested "Bill" Williams for assault after he beat up the woman posing as his wife. Williams ran a brothel on Salina Street and assaulted the woman for failing to turn over the proceeds of her night's work. The woman was not named in the account given in the *Central City Courier* newspaper.

Somehow, it all seemed harmless in the era before AIDS/HIV, and yet in many ways, prostitution was as much slavery as the chains that held men and women like William Henry. Gangsters like Charles "Lucky" Luciano made millions of dollars from women like Phebie Empie and Ruby Larkin only to toss the women aside when they were no longer of use. It is a trend that continues to this day.

Chapter 6

MAKING MONEY THE OLD-FASHIONED WAY

I 'll admit that this chapter's title comes from a tag line for a financial firm. Show me a city that has never had a dishonest politician, and I'll show you a nonexistent city. Someone once defined an honest politician as one who stays bought after being bought. Syracuse has had its share of political giants willing and able to throw their weight behind a project if suitable recompense was made available. Unfortunately, greed is a part of life, and politicians are not exempt from this all-too-human failing. Given the positions they hold, many times they are not brought to trial for their malfeasance.

Benjamin Roscoe was trusted by the city of Syracuse. After all, you don't hand the purse strings for the city to just anyone. You give that kind of financial control to a man you can trust, a man of impeccable reputation—a man like Benjamin Roscoe. And yet in 1890, Syracuse's treasurer found himself being tried for bribery. Prosecutors claimed money drawn from Roscoe's bank was used to bribe Alderman Charles E. Candee.[6] Roscoe's lawyer disagreed, stating that the money in question was used to purchase a trotter, a horse used in harness racing. In his opening, Assistant District Attorney Shore stated, "We will show the defendant offered $3,000 to Alderman Charles E. Candee with intent to influence his vote. It makes no difference in law or morals whether the bribe is taken or not." Like many investigations, this one started small and blossomed. The trial was quick, and Roscoe was acquitted of the charges. The jury believed the defense's claim of a possible horse purchase, and Roscoe did in fact buy the trotter later for $2,500. The prosecution's case was not helped by Candee's faulty memory.

Later that year, Charles Candee, the alderman Roscoe was accused of bribing, would feature in another political corruption trial—only this time he was the guest of honor. On December 26, 1890, Alderman Charles E. Candee was charged with wrongfully obtaining and receiving money belonging to the city with intent to defraud and with falsely impersonating another. The last charge comes from the alderman drawing money in the name of Thomas C. Drennan. Candee claimed that Drennan authorized him to use his name. Drennan did not refute the claim but added that it had been four or five years previous, when Drennan and

Syracuse City Hall. *Courtesy of Neil K. MacMillan.*

Candee had been partners in a business venture. Candee was specifically charged with defrauding the City of Syracuse of $168.00, including a $76.50 livery bill. Other city officials were named in connection with the trial, including Aldermen John McLennan and Frank Matty. Put briefly, a $76.50 livery bill opened a can of worms for the City of Syracuse and its aldermen. Both Candee and Alderman McLennan were exonerated by the grand jury.

Frank Matty was a mover and shaker, both in the Democratic Party and in the city of Syracuse. A cooper and tavern keeper before entering politics, Matty considered himself a realist who knew how the game was played. Given the rough-and-tumble nature of Gilded Age politics, it is not surprising that allegations of political malfeasance would crop up during his career. Indeed, charges of political skullduggery seemed to follow Matty throughout his career. Allegations of bribery cropped up when he was elected president of the board of aldermen. Twenty-eight-year-old James McGuire, known as the "boy mayor" because of his youth, was an implacable political foe of Matty and saw the alderman as the personification of all that was wrong with the political system in the city of Syracuse.

The honorable James K. McGuire, the "boy mayor" of Syracuse, was a staunch opponent of Frank Matty in the late 1890s. *Courtesy of the Library of Congress.*

On April 28, 1896, in an open message sent to the mayor of the Syracuse Common Council and published in the *Syracuse Daily Standard*, James K. McGuire accused Alderman Matty of attempting to coerce the Onondaga Lake Railroad Company into paying $7,000 to put the franchise proposal through the Syracuse Common Council. Matty vehemently refuted the charges. The grand jury refused to indict Matty on the bribery charges, but in September 1897, the State of New York Excise Department sued Matty for violating the liquor law.

Frank Matty retired from Syracuse politics in 1900. It is likely in today's climate that Matty would have done jail time. The politician retired to his farm on Brewerton Road in what is now the hamlet of Mattydale. He was instrumental in establishing the hamlet as well as the Mattydale Fire Department. Both the hamlet and Matty Avenue are named after him. Frank Matty died on February 10, 1939, leaving both a legacy of accomplishment and hints of political scandal.

These days, if a person wants a job in government—be it state, federal or local—he takes a civil service exam. If he passes it with a high enough score and there is a suitable position available, he gets hired. Qualifications have to be met. During the first decade of the twentieth century, government employment was a boon often offered to loyal political supporters. No one who picked up a newspaper in the last decades of the nineteenth century or the first decades of the twentieth would have been shocked by that fact. Today, the superintendent of schools is looked upon as a position of trust, as well it should be. In 1904, however, the superintendent of schools for Syracuse, Dr. Edward L. Mooney, was under indictment for bribery.

Miss May Spring dreamed of teaching children, and to realize that dream, she applied with the Syracuse school district. Like many wide-eyed youths of her day, Spring assumed all she needed was the desire to teach and the education to do so. Imagine her dismay when she was informed the privilege to teach in Syracuse schools would cost her $300! The people's case against Dr. Mooney, in a nutshell, alleged that he asked to be paid that amount for employing Miss Spring.

Was Dr. Mooney paid? The fact is that he was. His defense was that it was a loan from former alderman Frank Matty. Miss Spring and Commissioner of Public Safety Charles Listman countered that it was payment to secure Miss Spring's employment. The trial was held in Rochester, New York. Miss Spring testified that Listman told her she would have to pay the $300 to Dr. Mooney to be appointed. She added that she gave the note to Listman, who had it placed in the Salt Springs Bank. In the course of over a year, Mooney was tried twice and dismissed as superintendent of schools after being subjected to the school board's investigation. The culprit in all of this was none other than the former commissioner of public safety, Charles Listman. Under cross examination, Listman admitted that he was the originator of the alleged bribe and that Mooney knew nothing of it until the check showed up in his bank. Mooney was acquitted after Matty testified that he had indeed loaned Mooney $300 and on Listman's admission of bribery and perjury. The school board hired Miss Spring.

What are we to make of the four cases I describe? In all of them, the defendants were exonerated. Did they do it? In Mooney's case, it is fairly clear that he did not. Politics in the Gilded Age was no game for the faint of heart. With the reforms that have come along in the intervening 107 years since Dr. Mooney was tried and acquitted, the days of political patronage and bribery as the cost of doing business with city government are thankfully gone. The trials I cite here are as much Syracuse history as Ephraim Webster's agreement with the Onondaga nation for his famous square mile of land. To forget that is to open the door for yet another era of shady deals in the guise of good government.

Chapter 7

"BUD" AND "MOMSIE"

One might be forgiven for thinking that nothing happened in Syracuse in 1927. Prohibition was the law of the land, Sacco and Vanzetti were on trial for their lives in Boston and Charles Lindbergh had yet to make his historic flight across the Atlantic Ocean. Spring was just around the corner, and on March 18, no one in the city dreamed Syracuse would play part in a murder case that would make national headlines.

Ruth Snyder was tall, buxom and married to Albert Snyder. From all accounts, in spite of the fact that the couple had a child together, Ruth enjoyed keeping company with other men. The voluptuous would-be flapper spent few nights in the company of her daughter and husband, whom she referred to as the "old crab." When daughter Lorraine was at school, she entertained delivery boys. For his part, Albert kept a picture of his former fiancée above the marriage bed and referred to her in Ruth's presence as "the finest woman he had ever known." Ruth was competing with the ghost of her husband's now-deceased first lover.

But into Ruth's life came Henry Judd Gray, a dapper, stylish dresser and a corset salesman. The New Jersey native was married and had an eleven-year-old daughter, but that didn't stop him from entering into an affair with Ruth. The myopic Gray was a weak man, and Ruth called the shots during their two-year romance. She called Gray her "lover boy" or "Bud," and he called her "Momsie."

Marriage and motherhood were boring to Ruth. In 1926, the Queen's Village, Long Island housewife took out a $100,000 life insurance policy on

Albert. From that point on, Albert Snyder's days were numbered. Momsie made several attempts on her husband's life. Albert had no clue that his wife was plotting his demise. Frustrated with her lack of success, Ruth brought Henry Gray into the plot. Gray at first refused, but Momsie was nothing if not strong willed. Bud might have had qualms about murder, but he could not stand up to his indomitable lover. He argued against the murder to no avail. Ruth wanted Albert dead, and one way or another, she would get her way. Gray finally gave in.

On March 19, 1927, Gray, known as Judd to his family, arrived in Long Island after a morning of selling corsets in Syracuse. He meandered around the Snyders' neighborhood drinking from two bottles of bootleg whiskey in hope of being arrested as a drunk or for violating the Volstead Act. It didn't work. Around 2:00 a.m., he crept into the Snyder house through a back door Ruth had left unlocked.

After meeting Ruth, the couple made their way to Albert's bedroom, where Ruth handed Gray a sash weight. Bud brought the sash weight down on Albert's head, but the blow only roused Mr. Snyder. The doomed man grabbed Gray, who shrieked, "Momsie, Momsie! For God's sake, help!" Ruth did just that. She clubbed the sash weight down on her husband's head, knocking him unconscious. Momsie then took the hated picture of her husband's dead flame and used the wire it hung by to strangle Albert. On Momsie's orders, Bud then soaked a rag with chloroform and placed it over Albert's face, spilling so much that it burned the flesh. He then tied and gagged Ruth to make the crime look like a burglary gone horribly wrong.

The lovers' plan quickly became unraveled. Their attempts to cover up the crime were so inept that author Damon Runyon labeled them the "Dumbbell Murderers." Judd Gray made his way to Syracuse, where friends provided an alibi. Syracuse police arrested Gray on March 21 at the Onondaga Hotel. Two friends of Gray were arrested, charged with aiding Gray after the murder. Haddon Gray and Harry Platt, both of Syracuse, were accused of providing an alibi for Gray. The alibi, such as it was, was shattered when police found Gray's Pullman ticket in his hotel room. Police chief Martin L. Cadin called Gray "the coolest man I ever dealt with when accused of such a crime."[7] But for the police discovery of the shredded rail ticket, Gray's alibi might have held up.

Brought to trial, the couple wasted no time trying to throw the other under the bus. Ruth Snyder painted Gray as the evil mastermind behind the murder of Albert. Gray painted himself as a love slave manipulated into murder by Ruth Snyder. There may have been truth in that. The jury

The electrocution chamber in Sing Sing in 1915, where thirteen years later, Ruth Snyder and Judd Gray would pay the ultimate price for murder. *Courtesy of the Library of Congress.*

deliberated only for one hour and thirty-eight minutes. Both Ruth and Gray were convicted and sentenced to die in the electric chair. The couple was executed on the night of January 12, 1928. Gray went first in keeping with Sing Sing's tradition of executing the weaker of the conspirators first. A *New York Daily News* photographer who snuck a small camera into the execution chamber photographed Ruth Snyder at the moment of her execution. Subsequently, all persons witnessing executions were searched.

Though not the scene of the infamous murder, Syracuse police played a significant role in bringing Henry Judd Gray to justice. Within two years of Ruth Snyder's execution, the flapper craze would die out. Did her demise signal its end? Likely not. The Roaring Twenties gave way to the Great Depression. Syracuse moved on. Other stories took center stage from Bud and Momsie.

Chapter 8

FALLEN HEROES:
DETECTIVE HARVEY, PATROLMAN NEAR,
PATROLMAN HANNON AND OFFICER JARMACZ

We expect the police to be there when we need them. We may carp about them not pursuing "real" criminals when they pull us over for speeding or running that pesky red light, but they're on the job twenty-four hours a day, seven days a week. Syracuse doesn't come readily to mind when we think of cop killers. That happens in the big cities like Chicago, Los Angeles or New York. But, in fact, it does happen in Syracuse. In the period between 1893 and 1950, seven Syracuse policemen died in the line of duty. Three of them were murdered. The men and women of the Syracuse Police Department have a tradition of valor in the face of danger, and my choosing of Detective Harvey, Patrolmen Near and Hannon and Officer Jarmacz in no way diminishes the courage of the other police officers who have given their lives in the performance of their duties.[8]

The day threatened rain but was generally fair, as might be expected on the last day of July 1893 in Syracuse. Canadian-born detective James Harvey was on rounds when he was notified that there were two men acting suspiciously in Palmer's Government Café. Harvey suspected the men of committing a string of safe robberies and followed the men from the café on East Water Street. The sixty-three-year-old detective quickly took the two men into custody but failed to search them. While escorting them to the station, one of the suspects struck Harvey with a revolver. The other then pulled his own weapon and shot Harvey in the head. The murder occurred at about 10:10 a.m. in one of the busiest sections of Syracuse. The two suspects made off. George A. Barnes was chased and quickly

"All the cool miscreants are wearing them." Manacles and leg irons were used to limit the movements of prisoners in the nineteenth century. *Courtesy of Neil K. MacMillan.*

apprehended, found crouching under a stoop on Lock Street. The other suspect, Charles F. Wilson, was arrested in Buffalo, New York, giving his name as George Calhoun. Barnes was actually Lucius R. "Dink" Wilson, and the two killers were brothers. The brothers were notorious burglars and were known to the Pinkerton Detective Agency and various police departments throughout the country. The brothers were convicted of first-degree murder, and their request for a new trial was denied. Lucius R. Wilson was executed at Auburn Prison, while Charles was sentenced to life. The brothers had been outlaws in the West. "Dink" had ridden with the Hedgepeth gang before coming to Syracuse.

It should have been a routine call. Though prohibition was in full force in January 1923, Patrolman Pierson C. Near responded to a complaint about a drunk and disorderly patron at the Home Restaurant at 309 East Genesee Street. While Patrolman Near struggled to place James McCafferty in custody, Michael McCafferty took Near's revolver from the policeman's pocket and fired. McCafferty's first shot went wild, but the second lodged beneath Near's heart. The patrolman died an hour later. McCafferty fled to his sister's house in Eastwood, where he was apprehended five hours later. He confessed to shooting Near but claimed he had no intention of hurting or killing the policeman. Rather, he claimed he was driven to it by seeing Patrolman Near getting the best of his brother. Michael McCafferty was convicted and sentenced to twenty years in prison for second-degree murder.

Six years later, Patrolman James Hannon was walking his beat and checking doors to the businesses in his bailiwick. He discovered the rear door to the Walker Pharmacy ajar. He went to a nearby police phone and called his sergeant at the Beech Street precinct to notify him of the burglary. Upon returning to the store, Hannon arrested Harold Pickard. As he did so, William McKenna fired a shot that struck Patrolman Hannon in the elbow. The two suspects escaped, but Hannon managed to write down the license plate number of their vehicle. Hannon died of a heart attack while undergoing reconstructive surgery on his elbow.

Pickard pleaded guilty to a burglary charge and received a five- to ten-year sentence in Auburn prison. McKenna was questioned by Syracuse police while serving time in Massachusetts for another crime. He confessed to being involved with the burglary and to shooting Patrolman Hannon.

Patrolman John S. Jarmacz saw a lot in his twenty-nine years. A veteran, he saw action in Italy and the Pacific Theater as a military policeman. On

A paddy wagon from the early 1950s. *Courtesy of Peggy Reilly.*

August 30, 1947, Jarmacz fell off a transport wagon while struggling with a prisoner and was killed.

The Syracuse Police Department continues to combat crime in the tradition of the brave policemen who gave their lives in service to the city of Syracuse and its people.

Chapter 9

TODDY STRICKEN:
DEMON RUM AND PROHIBITION

Governments sometimes enact unpopular laws. The U.S. government flirted with Prohibition in the early twentieth century but didn't get serious about it until the breakout of World War I. Upon America's entry into the war, the U.S. Navy officially did away with the rum ration aboard naval vessels. Several states had already passed laws outlawing the sales of liquor for anything other than medicinal or industrial use. Maine had been dry since before the Civil War. The dreams of the temperance movement came to fruition in October 1919, when the Volstead Act was passed over President Wilson's veto and ratified as a constitutional amendment. That the Volstead Act was unpopular should surprise no one—nor should the fact that it was almost impossible to effectively enforce. But that wouldn't stop the feds or the Syracuse police from trying. The law may well have been the most hated act passed in the country's history.

In an ideal world, Prohibition would have worked. In our world, however, the Volstead Act proved not only unenforceable but also a boon to the nascent organized crime families. It is doubtful that Al Capone would have been a household name without the Volstead Act. Let's face it—people wanted their nightly cocktail. Demon rum became big business, and because it was illegal, people like Al Capone controlled that business. Syracuse didn't give rise to nationally famous gangsters, but the Salt City wasn't exactly as pure as the driven snow when it came to the Volstead Act. The police and federal authorities did their best to stem the spate of illegal hooch, but the flow of alcohol had a life of its own.

In 1917, Hampton Roads was a major training facility for new sailors. That year, the U.S. Navy abolished the rum ration, and liquor was no longer served on naval ships. *Courtesy of the Library of Congress.*

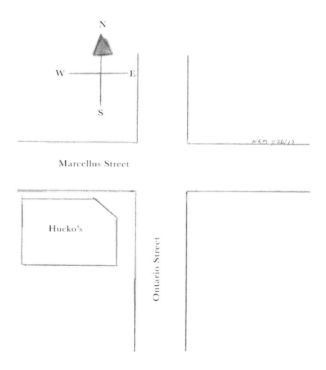

Map (not to scale) showing the location of Andrew Hucko's restaurant. *Courtesy of Neil K. MacMillan.*

Andrew Hucko owned a restaurant at 701 Marcellus Street at the Ontario Street intersection. On April 26, 1928, federal authorities raided his establishment and uncovered a cache of whiskey. Hucko was quickly arrested. He was convicted and sentenced in December 1930 and was

given a choice of serving four months with a federal road gang, sixty days in the Cayuga County jail and a $600 fine or thirty days and an $800 fine. The road gang was a novel approach in New York. John Bristo, who was sentenced along with Hucko, was given the choice of a $1 fine or a day in jail. Sentences were dramatically varied. It is not known if Bristo was a first-time offender. The building that was Hucko's restaurant still stands.

In an early test of state law, George and Michael Pappas were evicted from the storefront they rented from Syracuse University for violating the Volstead Act. Though George was convicted of violating New York State's Mullin-Gage Law, he was not convicted of violating the Volstead Act. The Volstead Act contained a provision allowing landlords to evict tenants if they were convicted of violating the act. The 1922 legal battle came about because the university evicted the brothers based on federal law. The brothers maintained that an outsider had brought liquor into the candy store and that it was not theirs. Pappas maintained that the two acts were distinctly different. Pappas was arrested after neighbors alleged that they had seen drunken college students leaving the Cosmopolitan Candy Store. Syracuse detectives of the Prohibition Enforcement Squad alleged that they found three different types of wine at Pappas's establishment.

Legal challenges to the Volstead Act plagued courts throughout its thirteen-year existence. One of the many challenges concerned who had power to enforce the law. On the evening of Saturday, November 17, 1923, police raided Frank McLaughlin's store after neighbors made allegations of gambling being permitted on the premises. When the raid was executed, detectives spotted a bottle that Frank McLaughlin had emptied into the sink. Police used a sponge to soak up the evidence, and a charge of violating the Volstead Act was issued. No evidence of gambling was found. McLaughlin's lawyers argued that a warrant should have been issued and that the method of gathering the evidence had corrupted the evidence. The detectives countered that the bottle was in plain sight while raiding the establishment for another crime. During the court hearings, the federal government maintained that any possession of alcoholic beverages was illegal except in the narrow strictures of the Volstead Act. Oliver Burden, the U.S. attorney hearing the complaint, ruled that the police acted in good faith and would have been guilty of dereliction had they not arrested McLaughlin.[9]

On a blustery February night in 1929, police raided the exclusive Saengerbund Club. The club's membership included many of the city's elite. Police Chief Harry McWayne led the raid after complaints from neighbors alleged numerous violations of the Volstead Act. Police smashed through two locked doors after obtaining a search warrant based on the testimony of an undercover operative. Several quarts of gin, a quart of wine, a gallon of hard cider and two cases of Canadian ale were seized, and the club's officers were charged with violating the Volstead act. The club was located at the corner of Oswego and Seymour Streets.

Upon taking office, President Franklin D. Roosevelt signed a bill repealing the Volstead Act, and states quickly ratified the amendment repealing prohibition. Many luminaries in the nation were opposed to the law, including

A variety of pre–Prohibition era liquor bottles in the author's collection. *Courtesy of Neil K. MacMillan.*

Roosevelt, a former governor of New York State, and Governor Al Smith, the first Roman Catholic candidate for president. In point of fact, many of the same congressmen that voted for the Volstead Act kept spirituous liquors in their chambers. The dreams of the temperance societies ended up being just that—dreams. Prohibition did not make for a better society. As I stated above, it gave a huge boost to organized crime, creating household names of the likes of Al Capone. Many otherwise law-abiding citizens saw it as unwarranted government intrusion into their personal lives. In addition, scores of people were killed, blinded or suffered medical complications drinking poisonous "bathtub gin."[10] With the end of Prohibition came new taxes on liquor and beer and regulations on production and sales. Liquor now had to be bonded to ensure its quality. But the end of Prohibition did not signal the demise of organized crime. Rather, the syndicate moved into other areas of criminal enterprise. Syracuse emerged from Prohibition and moved forward.

Chapter 10

BAD TRIPS:
ILLEGAL DRUGS IN THE CITY

I t is hard to believe that 108 years ago, you could walk into a drugstore and buy cocaine-laced medicinal products. New York State law required labeling products containing cannabis under poison control statutes in place from the 1860s. It was legal to possess marijuana until the passage of the Marihuana Tax Act in 1937.[11] The war on drugs has been one of occasional victory marred by sometimes-monumental setbacks. Though prior to the mid-1960s, drug possession didn't garner the sort of attention it does these days, it was still in the news and concerned many citizens. A case could be made that the initial outcry against narcotics had racial overtones. Chinese immigrants were blamed for bringing the habit of smoking opium to the United States. Opiates had been used for decades throughout the world for relief of pain after surgery. In point of fact, many soldiers injured in the Civil War, Indian Wars and the War with Spain returned home with a morphine addiction. Opiates were consumed for a variety of ills in the form of laudanum or in patent medicines.

How did Syracuse deal with drug offenses in the period between 1907 and 1950? Let's look at a few cases throughout that period, shall we? Then as now, drug possession was a federal offense, and while in recent years some states have decriminalized marijuana use, the federal government has not. Drug use and trafficking was seen as a large and growing problem. We may have advanced past the days of Reefer Madness, but the social concerns are still there, as evidenced by the stories on the news.

As early as 1919, law enforcement agents noted with alarm the increasing flow of drugs across the Mexican border. It was estimated that drug users were paying $10 million a day for their high. It was also believed that the enforcement of Prohibition led to increases in drug use and trafficking. These days, it is not uncommon to hear of huge drug raids and trials, but they are not unique to the twenty-first century, as a huge trial was held in Syracuse in November 1928. Twenty-six defendants were charged with drug offenses, and

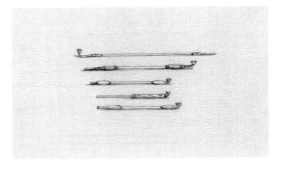

Meji-period Japanese drawing of opium pipes, circa 1878. Though opium was legal in the United States and in Syracuse at the time, it would later be criminalized for general use. Opiates still play a medicinal role in pain management. *Courtesy of the Library of Congress.*

police expected that the raid dried up a sizeable portion of the drug trade in the city. Among the indicted were William A. "Yellow" Burns, noted for being overly familiar with the inside of a jail cell and boxer Al Fisher and his wife, who accused Fisher of introducing her to dope. Herbert Titus, a notorious narcotics peddler, was also swept up in the massive raid. It was estimated at the time that the twenty-six defendants were responsible for bringing in 75 percent of the morphine, cocaine and heroin in the city.

Syracuse and federal officials launched a major push in July 1937 to crack down on people getting narcotics by fraudulent prescription. Among those arrested was Dr. Norman Foster, an oculist charged with violating the Harrison Act by prescribing narcotics to known addicts. Major Garland Williams, the chief federal narcotics enforcement officer for New York, believed that eliminating fraudulent prescriptions by doctors would eliminate the narcotics problem in Syracuse. Marijuana was considered the major menace in the area.

Police Chief Martin Cadin had a mission in the fall of 1920—he was determined to drive all illicit drug users from Syracuse. Certainly it was, and still is, a lofty goal. Among his targets that November was August Rini, better known as "Checkers." Rini was arrested with approximately $10,000 worth of narcotics. In addition, Cadin moved to arrest all known addicts in the city. Police also arrested Jerry Luco, whom they described as the "mastermind" behind the drug ring. Both Luco and Rini were from Rochester, and their arrests showed that even in the early days of the war on drugs there was an intra-city organization in full swing.

A year later, police arrested Joseph Capharie for drug smuggling. They alleged that Capharie was bringing in morphine and cocaine from Canada. He had two ounces of drugs valued at $750 in 1921. They also alleged that he used a network of young boys, many who were addicts themselves, to distribute the drugs. Syracuse officials estimated that as many as one hundred addicts had returned to their illicit use after treatment and were getting their fix from Capharie.

Chief Cadin's efforts proved to take much longer than he expected. Twenty years later, local and federal law enforcement agents arrested two Syracusans with four others as part of a raid in Auburn, New York. The Syracuse couple, Mr. and Mrs. Stopyra of Hawley Avenue, was charged with obtaining narcotics through fraud. Mr. Stopyra pleaded guilty; his wife pleaded not guilty. They were convicted. Mr. Stopyra's sentence was suspended on the condition that he undergo treatment for addiction. Mrs. Stopyra's case was adjourned until the following Monday. The problem of fraudulent prescriptions continues to this day, accompanied by theft of prescription pads.

If you're going to violate one law, why not shoot the works? A car was seized in October 1928 after state police on horseback noticed that the springs were sagging. They pulled the car over at gunpoint. The driver dashed into the woods and made his escape. The gentleman in question was smuggling in champagne and had an opium pipe and a quantity of opium in the car. Police investigators subsequently dismantled the New York City vehicle in the course of their job.

These days, we tend to look at the 1950s as a time of bucolic innocence. The period was one that spoke of a white-bread world in which crime was a distant thing—or at least that's how it was portrayed on television. We simply don't think of drugs when we think of 1950. Enter John Martin. Martin was rushed to Memorial Hospital with symptoms of a drug overdose. Arrested by Syracuse police, Martin was arraigned and pleaded guilty to violating the Public Health Law. The cause of his downfall was a hypodermic needle that tested positive for traces of morphine and cocaine.

The argument has been put forth that drug abuse is a victimless crime and has almost as quickly been dismantled by the weight of evidence. In 1933, burglars broke into a post office substation and stole cash, quantities of government liquor and morphine valued at several hundred dollars. In these days, when drug cartels wage war against each other and the yearly body counts are in the hundreds if not thousands, these crimes may seem trivial. But one should bear in mind that these early crimes represent the birth of the drug crime problem. That addiction existed before drugs were outlawed by the several acts that states and federal government enacted is indisputable. Would society be better served if narcotics were available to everyone without criminal penalty? That is a question best answered by experts. Obviously, illicit drugs are big business for criminal enterprises and will continue to be so until their demand is no longer there.

Chapter 11

"THAT'S WHERE THE MONEY IS": BANK ROBBERY

A reporter once asked notorious 1940s and '50s bank robber Willie Sutton why he robbed banks. Sutton, a wit as well as a bank robber, answered, "That's where the money is." Banks were being robbed before Willie was in this world, and they will continue to be robbed long after we are gone for that very reason. Sutton was a subtle robber who never carried a gun. However, John Dillinger and others of his ilk carried weapons, and some were not averse to using them.

In 1934, Syracuse and New York State Police arrested a dapper young man in Mattydale, New York. His name was Lonnie[12] Parish, and he styled himself "Dillinger the Second." Convicted of bank robbery in Patterson, Georgia, Parish escaped prison and made his way to the Syracuse suburb of Mattydale. His partner in the bank robberies, Harry Brown Gainey, was also nabbed in the raid. The wives of the two bank robbers were held as material witnesses. The quartet on the lam might not have been apprehended had not police been called about an alleged illegal still, for which Parish and Gainey were held in the Jamesville penitentiary awaiting extradition. At one point, Gainey was transferred to the Cedar Street Jail in Syracuse to be treated for an infected wound. In a twist not found these days, State Trooper William Blackburn Jr. successfully sued to receive the $9,000 in reward money offered for the capture of Parish and Gainey. The two alleged bank robbers fought extradition on the grounds that they were not positively identified as the Georgia bank robbers.

The 1938 robbery of the First Trust Bank in the Chimes Building, located at 500 South Salina Street, was the second largest in Syracuse history. In that era, thugs were usually heavily armed with semi-automatic .45 pistols and Thompson submachine guns. But the Syracuse bank was robbed not by desperadoes sporting massive firepower but by con men. The four suspects in the Chimes Building robbery lifted the cash by reaching through an adjacent teller window while the teller went to answer a phone call. By January 11, 1940, three of the four suspects were in custody. Royal Steinberg, William O. Evans and Frederick Kearns were indicted on federal bank robbery charges.[13]

The robbery of the F.W. Edwards department store, which occurred on July 20, 1924, was the record to break. Safe crackers, known in criminal parlance as "yeggs," tied up guard John McClarity and blew open the safe. They made off with $25,000 in cash and jewelry. The guard was handcuffed to a pipe in a restroom but managed to get free and notify a passerby, who in turn notified police. Police chief Martin Cadin believed they were professional safecrackers who had help from someone who knew the layout of the store and their way around Syracuse. One of the few clues in the case concerned a woman who may have been involved. After six months, the robbery remained unsolved. In December 1924, New York police arrested two men who they hoped would have ties to the Syracuse heist. It was believed that Fred Conley was the mastermind behind the robbery. Conley was arrested in June 1927 in Detroit to face burglary and jail-breaking charges. The twenty-six-year-old Conley, who wore what kids today would call Harry Potter glasses, pleaded guilty to stealing furs and diamonds from

The Syracuse Savings Bank building (now Bank of America) as seen from Clinton Square. *Courtesy of Neil K. MacMillan.*

Oswald's store to the tune of $15,000. He was sentenced to eleven years and six months in Auburn Prison.

Llewellyn B. Winslow appeared to be an upstanding citizen. The insurance salesman seemed like an ordinary guy, and yet on an August afternoon in 1947, armed with a toy cap pistol, he strolled into a First Trust bank branch office and attempted to rob the teller by forcing payment on a bogus check. The teller did not hand over the cash, and Winslow was arrested a few hours later. Confined by grand jury action, Winslow threatened to commit suicide, leading the court to have him evaluated for mental illness. He was judged sane.

While the period before 1950 may appear sparse for bank robbery in Syracuse, bear in mind that other crimes plagued the city, and Syracuse police were involved in apprehending miscreants who robbed banks elsewhere, as the Parish/Gainey case shows. Criminals would make up for their lack of attention to Syracuse banks after 1950.

Chapter 12

THE WEIRD AND UNUSUAL:
CRIMES OF THE HEART

What makes for an unusual crime? Perhaps it is something that was once illegal but no longer is, although that is really too broad a definition in my opinion. It has to stand out and make you ask, "Are they serious?" It might be humorous or tragic, but it will be weird even for the time it occurred. Let's face it—love is messy and sometimes fickle. If you're going to marry someone, it's probably a good idea to not be married to someone else at the time. You should also be careful of what you promise, as it might get you in trouble with the law.

We don't usually think of preachers as Lotharios. The image of an evangelist conjures up pictures of devotion and staid, stern attention to the duties imposed by God. Imagine then the dismay of the members of the Elmwood Presbyterian Church when their young minister was named in a breach-of-promise suit. Ervin T. Liddle was a recently married young minister and self-styled evangelist. That he married Lydia Stead legally was never in question. The problem was that he had apparently promised to marry two other women as well. Needless to say, these two women were neither amused nor entertained when they discovered he had married Miss Stead. One of the scorned lovers, Miss Nettie Williams, came to Syracuse intent on suing the good reverend for breach of promise and to recoup monies borrowed from her by Liddle. Miss Williams would have pressed the suit, but the state of the clergyman's finances convinced her that she would not recoup her losses. Another of the evangelist's erstwhile fiancées substantiated Miss Williams's claims. Miss Jessie Palmer was also engaged to Ervin T. Liddle and stated that

The Path of Least Resistance. This *Puck* magazine cover shows young lovers sharing a tender moment. Could this have led to a breach-of-promise suit? *Courtesy of the Library of Congress.*

she and Liddle were to have wed in April 1898. I have to wonder what the newly minted Mrs. Liddle thought of all this.

Ernest D. Tyler found out that upsetting your fiancée's sister is not a good idea. It becomes an even worse idea when you mention marrying someone else. By law, Tyler was married, but he claimed that in serving a sentence for bigamy, he was let out of his first marriage. He also stated that his second marriage was "null and void." Ernest had told Miss Lillian Armstrong that he intended to runaway with and marry her sister Jennie, although he was still legally married to his second wife, Margaret Gill. The judge advised him to let his lawyer handle any further attempts at defense.

Comedians joke about their marriages, and even ordinary guys complain about the pitfalls inherent in marriage. Howard Richardson didn't listen. Richardson's first marriage, to Catherine Scanlon Richardson, ended in divorce. As part of the divorce agreement, Howard was not to marry again without obtaining permission of the court beforehand. The first Mrs. Richardson drove a hard bargain. Married only a year, Catherine was granted the divorce in 1921. Howard, being the romantic sort, married again in 1927 to Agnes, the second Mrs. Richardson. But it seems that Howard neglected to gain the court's permission to marry Agnes and to tell Agnes about the divorce. Oops! Agnes was just a little peeved. Howard was arrested for bigamy in 1929. The charges were dropped when Catherine Richardson could not be located to contest the marriage. The Richardsons' marriage was troubled almost from the beginning, as Agnes had previously been arrested for assaulting Howard. The monastery might have been a better idea, Howard.

We don't hear much about breach of promise these days. In 1935, suits for breach of promise became increasingly rare, as the United States government limited them. Perhaps not so ironically, diamond rings began to be more commonplace. The rings offered the prospective bride some measure of financial security. The relaxing of sexual mores in the 1920s basically sounded the death knell for breach-of-promise torts in this country.

Another crime of yesteryear was seduction. These days, we may bemoan our sons and daughters having sexual intercourse before they are of the age of consent—and rightly so. We may question their choices, but their seduction is not illegal unless they are below the age of consent. Things were different in the early days of the twentieth century. The period before the Roaring Twenties offered many hazards for the would-be Lothario. In a day when there are few consequences for seduction, barring sexually transmitted diseases or pregnancy, it is almost incomprehensible that people could go to jail for sex without the benefits of holy matrimony. Seduction, like breach of promise, was one of those crimes that held sway in both criminal and civil court. It was an era when a girl's prospects were much improved if she was chaste. It was all about climbing the social ladder or maintaining or bettering one's position on said ladder.

Consider if you will, the case of Charles E. Kearney, who in June 1887 faced both civil and criminal charges for seducing Mary Carroll. The suit, brought by Mary's father, Peter, alleged that Kearney deprived Mr. Carroll of his daughter's services by seducing her. These days, the judge on the civil case would likely fine Mr. Carroll for wasting the court's valuable time. Charles Kearney was convicted. On appeal, the conviction was upheld.

In 1904, the Onondaga County Sheriff's Department was empowered to hear a breach-of-promise and seduction case against Charles Wehner Jr. Lena Walker charged that Mr. Wehner had seduced her and promised to marry her. The sheriff's jury awarded Walker $4,000 when Wehner failed to appear in court. At the time, it was rumored that Wehner fled to Germany.

These days, Henry A. Russell would be charged with statutory rape and child abuse. However, in 1886, he was charged with seducing his niece Hattie Benson. The complaint alleged that Russell had seduced the girl over a period of months while she visited her grandmother, who lived with Russell. The father asked for $5,000 in damages. Russell was arrested and given bail in the amount of $2,500, which he furnished. During the trial, Russell's attorney argued that Hattie's "reputation for veracity was very bad."[14] In addition, the girl's grandmother testified that Hattie had never complained to her of any improprieties taking place. The grandmother also testified that Hattie was unruly and that she could not be relied on to tell the truth, allegations that Hattie's stepmother resolutely refuted in her testimony. During the trial, police sought Hattie on a charge of truancy. Her parents maintained that she had been spirited away by the defendant's friends. She returned to her parents unharmed. On December 11, 1886, Henry Russell was convicted and ordered to pay damages to William Benson. I'm left with two questions about this case. Would Russell be convicted today? I suspect not. And having been convicted of what today amounted to child molestation, why didn't Russell go to jail? Perhaps the answer lies buried in the testimony. Certainly, the grandmother's testimony that her granddaughter's word was best taken with a grain of salt weighed with the jury. It is a troubling case for the incestuous aspects and the fact that the girl was well under what the age of consent would be these days—more proof that the Gilded Age wasn't the solid gold some believe it to have been.

Chapter 13

RANSOM AND RUIN: KIDNAPPING

Few crimes arouse more revulsion than kidnapping another human being. Most of us view the act as despicable, whether for monetary gain in the form of ransom, sexual gratification or as a hostage or bargaining chip for some misguided political agenda. Though penalties have stiffened over the years and our methods of locating and liberating victims and bringing the culprits to justice have improved, kidnapping remains a potent threat in these days of drug cartels and terrorist groups. Add to that the sometimes-bitter custody battles that rage when marriage goes horribly wrong, and kidnapping hangs over us like a specter. It is little wonder that penalties are severe.

Grace Lamphere was thirteen years old when she disappeared from her home in Little Falls, New York, in 1897. A year later, she was found working as a drudge in the house of Reverend Jervis Maybee. The Lamphere kidnapping was part of a larger scheme involving child brokerage. Maybee and his Confederates were kidnapping children and placing them in other homes for their own good. Bishop Ludden of the Syracuse Roman Catholic Diocese roundly damned the plan. Though it was stated that Grace enjoyed her time in Maybee's house, the facts were unequivocal on the point that she loathed her condition. Though many discounted accounts of white slavery as rumor, there is no doubt that Maybee kidnapped both Grace Lamphere and Daisy Millard. Neither the Lampheres nor Millards gave permission to the reverend to remove their daughters from their custody. Maybee's supporters considered his "work" a kindness on behalf of destitute children. Grace Lamphere and Daisy Millard were neither destitute nor abandoned. No matter what

A "Black Maria" with kidnappers. Though not taken in Syracuse, this photo gives a good representation of police transportation in the nineteenth and early twentieth centuries. *Courtesy of the Library of Congress.*

Maybee's motives were, his actions constituted kidnapping. That anyone could have seen his crime as altruism boggles the mind.

Kidnapping is and was a rare crime in Syracuse. When we think of the year 1949, we don't think of armed thugs robbing and kidnapping people on Syracuse's streets. Twenty-four-year-old advertising artist Norma Jean Acker and her companion Cecil Williams certainly never imagined that they would suffer that fate. In the early morning hours of June 17, 1949, Williams stopped his car for a man standing in the middle of the road. The man and his accomplice subsequently dragged Williams from the car and beat him unconscious. The assailants also robbed him of twenty dollars. When Williams awoke, Miss Acker was gone. After being dragged from the car, Norma Jean had a burlap sack placed over her head and was put in another car. She was released a little while later on Mountainview Avenue, not far from where the assault and kidnapping had occurred. Police arrested Patsy Senzarino and Angelo DeAngelo for the kidnapping, stating that they were part of a larger gang of men involved in the abduction. Both men were convicted. Senzarino was sentenced to a term of forty years to life, while DeAngelo was sentenced to a term of twenty years to life. Both were imprisoned in Attica Penitentiary.

Twenty years earlier, Herbert Canfield Jr. was arrested on charges of kidnapping, auto theft, halting an automobile and impersonating a federal agent. His accomplice, Clair Pingray, was indicted at the same time. In a bizarre twist, Herbert Canfield Sr. died on the day his son was arrested. The elder Canfield was suffering from ill health and had removed himself from Syracuse to Cuba Lake. His doctor surmised that the arrest hastened his death.

We have been fortunate in Syracuse not to suffer political kidnappings, and the other kidnappings I mention here seem to almost be spur of the moment, with the exception of the good Reverend Maybee. Still, no matter the motivation, the crime has always been both sinister and terrifying.

Chapter 14

MAKING MONEY THE OLD-FASHIONED WAY II:
COUNTERFEITING AND FORGERY

The government and politicians tell us they want us to *make* money, but what they really mean is that they want us to *earn* money. It is a small but important distinction. You see, making money will get you a stretch in the pokey. Through the antebellum period, banks were allowed to print their own money (as were the several states). With the advent of government-issued notes in the 1860s, printing your own money ranked right up there with coining your own double eagles.[15] In the case of printing your own money, it's much cheaper than coinage. People have been counterfeiting since governments have been making coins, and I suspect they will continue to for quite some time. In criminal law, to counterfeit is to make something false in the semblance of that which is true with fraudulent intent. Forgery covers a broad spectrum and can include documents, manuscripts and checks that don't belong to you, as well as making your own bank notes. During the Great Depression, several merchants in Syracuse's Eastwood neighborhood offered credit tokens. They were not charged with counterfeiting because they were never intended as legal currency. Rather, the tokens served as part of a barter system to help the community and merchants deal with the economic turmoil prostrating America at that time.

Harold Marquisee styled himself a doctor—at least that's what he told police he was when he was arrested. Unlike many forgers, Mr. Marquisee didn't forge stocks or bank notes. Instead, he counterfeited patent medicine trademarks, as patent medicines were big business in the 1890s. Arraigned for forgery and counterfeiting, Marquisee was tried and

A pair of patent medicine bottles from the author's collection. While the claims were outrageous for the "benefits" of these nostrums, one manufacturer, Lydia Pinkham, lives on in song. *Courtesy of Neil K. MacMillan.*

convicted. In April 1897, the Onondaga County court fined him $200 for the forgery. Marquisee was later charged with burglary and grand larceny and sentenced to three and a half years in Auburn Prison. In the indictment against him in Syracuse, Marquisee was charged with counterfeiting, forgery and grand larceny. After Marquisee was captured in Los Lobos, California, Oneida County sheriff Weaver went to Los Lobos and served a writ of extradition, bringing Marquisee back to New York to answer for crimes committed in Utica. Marquisee briefly escaped in Syracuse when he broke away from the arresting officer but was quickly chased down by citizens. He tried getting rid of coins that were found to be counterfeit. He was returned to Rome, New York, to stand trial for stealing a typewriter, and though that may seem like a trifling charge these days, typewriters were expensive machines in the 1890s. Utica police also found counterfeiting equipment in his offices.

Elmer Hattas and his brother-in-law, W. Emmett McHuron, wanted money. To get it, they allegedly passed forged notes to the Union Loan Association. The two men allegedly attempted to steal $25,000 with the bogus notes, which were supposedly endorsed by friends and relatives. Though charges were proffered in July 1897, Hattas wasn't arrested until March 2 the following year. W. Emmett McHuron was later arrested in Kansas City. Both men were charged with seventeen counts of forgery. Then as now, cases could be time consuming. McHuron was granted bail of $3,000, and his trial was postponed so that the defense could locate a witness. Much of the pair's forgery was aimed at McHuron's aunt. In April 1899, McHuron changed his plea to guilty, hoping for leniency from the court.

Compared to Hattas and McHuron, the four counterfeiters arrested by Secret Service agents in December 1934 were pikers. If you're going to get arrested for counterfeiting, $335 seems like a rather small amount of money. It just seems like a singular lack of work ethic for a federal rap. Samuel Lombardo, Carmen Carozza, Thomas Valerino and Rose Venturo were arrested in a drive against counterfeiters. Edith Carrelli was held as a material witness. The money, fake five- and ten-dollar notes, was discovered by detectives acting on tips about bogus bills being passed. Miss Venturo admitted passing several fake bills. Carozza claimed to have bought the bills for $35 from an unnamed man with the intention of passing them.

Shinplaster, a lithograph by H.R. Robinson. This note was not meant to be used as currency, a fact made obvious by the condemnation of the fiscal policies of Presidents Jackson and Van Buren. *Courtesy of the Library of Congress.*

The raid was part of a federal effort to roll up a ring of counterfeiters who were passing up to $2 million in fake greenbacks in New York and New Jersey. Valerino was arrested in Wayne County on a burglary charge and convicted in 1935. His appeal was denied. Samuel Lombardo was released in March 1935. Carozza was convicted and sentenced to five years in prison and fined $100. In a strange postscript, five years later, Thomas Valerino was exonerated in a charge of counterfeiting when his nephew Joseph confessed to passing bills received from a tall gray-haired man. He originally claimed that Thomas Valerino had passed the money to him.

With the advent of computers, forgery and counterfeiting entered a new era. In effect, the days of some guy whipping off a few twenties in his basement are gone. Detection methods have improved, but that doesn't mean that the days of counterfeiting and forgery are behind us. As long as governments print money, forgers and counterfeiters will be with us.

Chapter 15

MURDER MOST FOUL

Murder is the first crime mentioned in the Bible.[16] For some reason, we have a penchant for killing each other, which may be why it is also mentioned again in the Ten Commandments. People kill for a variety of reasons and will continue to do so. Murder wasn't quite as common in the 1800s as it is today in Syracuse. Perhaps it is instructive that in the period between 1840, when Zachariah Freeman was executed for killing his common-law wife, and 1890, when William Kemmler was electrocuted for killing his mistress, only four people were hanged in Onondaga County. But that doesn't mean there were only four murders. Murder has plagued Syracuse since the city's inception and will likely continue until the judgment trumpet sounds.

Twenty-one-year-old William Burns was drunk. He believed that the horse and carriage Alonzo Y. West and a gentleman name Blye were driving belonged to the Bangs and Gaynor livery. The two men offered to prove that the horses were indeed theirs and cajoled him into entering the carriage. During the ride, the duo allegedly tried to throw Burns from the carriage. During the struggle, Alonzo West was stabbed in the heart and died instantly. At first, the police believed that Burns used a dirk to stab West and that he had also carried a pistol. But the judge disallowed testimony by a gentleman by the name of Aitken to that effect. The prosecution, striving to prove first-degree murder, which would bring a sentence of death by hanging, was facing a severe difficulty. There was no doubt that Burns stabbed West to death. The question of motivation came to the fore. Burns agreed to confess

The electric chair at Auburn State Prison, first used in 1890 to electrocute William Kemmler. The electric chair was seen as more humane than hanging while still providing a deterrent to murder. *Courtesy of the Library of Congress.*

to second-degree murder. He told a reporter for the *Syracuse Standard* that he had rarely "been on a spree."[17] He added that he had never been that drunk. Burns was given life in Auburn Prison. He told the reporter that he was satisfied that he had been treated fairly. Today, it is very possible that Burns would have been acquitted on grounds of self-defense or given a minimal sentence for manslaughter.

In June 1865, as Syracuse troops were returning from the horrors of the Civil War to parades and the waiting embraces of their loved ones, Syracuse was reliving a brutal murder. Burr Burton had been a member of the New York State Assembly in 1856. In the early morning hours of May 3, 1865, he was shot during a break-in at his house on Danforth Street in Syracuse's First Ward. Hearing a suspicious noise, he arose and investigated. Assemblyman Burton called out, "Who's there?" He was answered by a pistol shot that pierced his lungs. He perished the next day. The mayor of Syracuse wasted no time in offering a $1,000 reward, and Burton's assassins were quickly arrested. The murderers were Michael Welsh and a man by the name of Daily,[18] who was also known as Thomas Johnson. Welsh was a career criminal who boasted that he had made $14,000 in 1864 without doing a day's work. In a day when a naval rear admiral made $3,000 to $5,000 a year, this was a heady boast, and if true, a very substantial fortune! Daily, twenty years old, was also a career criminal and a deserter from the Fifteenth New York Cavalry regiment. Welsh was living in New Orleans at the outbreak of the Civil War and was drafted into the Confederate army. He wasted no time deserting and continuing his antebellum avocation of burglary, riding out of Atlanta on a rail. He then migrated to Columbia, South Carolina, and barely escaped with his life after his sojourn there. He crossed into Maryland on a forged pass and made his way to Syracuse. Daily, from Durhamville in Oneida County, had pleaded guilty to larceny and was serving ten years of hard labor at Auburn when arraigned on the Burton murder. When arrested, he blamed the killing on Welsh. Daily claimed that Welsh broke out the pane of glass while attempting to "crack" the house and shot Burton when he came to investigate.

These days, when you pick up a paper or turn on the television, you will rarely see murder cases from outside your area unless they are particularly heinous. In the days before television and radio, however, murder was uncommon enough to warrant inclusion even if it occurred in a foreign country. In 1938, seventy-three years after the murder of Burr Burton, another case would focus Syracuse's attention, when Paducah, Kentucky native Laurence Gough murdered Laura Krenrich. The motive was not money, but like the Burns case, whiskey was involved. Gough admitted to drinking about a pint of whiskey with the victim. He stated that the victim made advances on him and asked him to do things he found "indecent and inhuman."[19] Afterward, he went to the kitchen, retrieved a pipe from a drawer and struck Laura Krenrich several times. He put her body in a cedar chest and attempted to sell her furniture but was unsuccessful. He sold some jewelry for twenty dollars. The thirty-one-year-old bartender/waiter was quickly extradited to Syracuse and charged with first-degree murder. Gough had been known as "Home-run Larry" while playing on his high school baseball team, and his father described him as a normal boy but was disturbed about his drinking. While in Paducah, Larry tried to get advice from his estranged wife. When she refused to talk to him, he turned himself in to Paducah police and confessed to killing Krenrich. Gough pleaded guilty to second-degree murder in the killing of Krenrich. Love and liquor didn't mix well in the Gough case.

Eighteen-year-old George F. Martin needed money. His solution? Robbery. He and his accomplices, Francis Gwilz and Robert Wilbur, killed Harold Berman while attempting to rob the victim's garage. Charged with murder in the first degree, Martin remained defiant throughout most of the trial. He confessed to killing Berman but maintained that he had no intention of killing the man. He was found guilty of second-degree murder and sentenced to twenty years to life in prison. His wife, Evelyn, vowed to remain faithful and to pray for his eventual release. Judge Williams stated that he did not believe Martin intended to kill Berman and hoped that he and his two co-defendants would learn from this experience and strive to become productive members of society again.

Murder happens for many different reasons. Indeed, as the three aforementioned cases show, the motives vary as much as the individuals involved. As I type this, the murder rate in Syracuse is approximately eighteen victims a year, many killed as a result of drug or gang violence. Others are the result of domestic violence, just as Laura Krenrich's murder was, while some are fueled by drink. Fortunately, murderers are quickly apprehended here as we move further into the twenty-first century.

Chapter 16

THE WEIRD AND UNUSUAL:
SOME PEOPLE WILL STEAL ANYTHING

W e've looked at bank robbery and other forms of larceny, but what about those cases that defy explanation? You know the ones I mean. The cases that make you ask, "They stole what? What were they thinking?" People will steal anything, and indeed, that is the whole point of this chapter. Having previously been employed as a store detective, I can vouch for that fact. How unusual can thievery get? Let's take a peek, shall we?

Apparently, Charles Root was cold. On May 5, 1865, Root stole an overcoat while in the Pinkerton and Popineau Saloon in the Weiting Block. He was arraigned before Justice Steven and pleaded guilty. He was offered the option of paying twenty-five dollars or serving ninety days in the penitentiary.

On January 23, 1920, Anton Blattner was arraigned on charges of theft. Blattner denied allegations that he had stolen two thousand pounds of sugar from a storage warehouse. I guess he had a sweet tooth. Arraigned the same day as Blattner, John McCall apparently wanted to make a clean sweep of things. McCall, who was on parole for a life sentence for committing habitual crimes, pleaded not guilty to stealing some brooms.

I wish I could say I made this next item up, but I didn't. In 1948, Levi B. Mead of Albany was charged with stealing sheets and pillowcases valued at less than fifty dollars from the Schenectady Distribution Depot. I'll wager that he didn't get to go to a minimum-security facility.

You'd think it was the Old West when Vernon Gebo and Ralph S. Dickinson of Syracuse were charged with grand larceny after they attempted

Syracuse isn't thought of as a center for cattle rustling, but that didn't stop Vernon Gebo and Ralph Dickinson from trying. *Courtesy of the Library of Congress.*

to steal a Guernsey bull and cow from Leslie Appleby's farm. Was milk really that expensive in the spring of 1946?

William Leo Wilcox was eclectic in his selection of other people's items. The twenty-five-year-old man was indicted for stealing $379 worth of appliances from the Firestone store, more than $500 worth of clothing from Associated Laundries, a doctor's medical case and instruments and $423 worth of silverware, compacts, linen and assorted other articles from a car. His attorney claimed that the man needed a psychiatric evaluation. I'm not sure I would disagree with the lawyer's assessment.

In 1950, Herbert Lang drew a thirty-day sentence for stealing a deck of playing cards from Woolworth's Department Store on Salina Street. The trial occurred April 11. This was a game of chance Herbert should have avoided.

In 1940, Sam Cicali and Clarence Moffitt pleaded guilty to petit larceny after stealing two stoves. Both received thirty days in the county lockup, but Cicali's sentence was suspended in consideration for his large family. Patrolman John Fogarty arrested the pair after following their truck's tire track in the snow. I guess they were cooking with gas.

Three youths were detained on October 3, 1945, after stealing twenty rolls of electrical tape from a Salvation Army store on South State Street.

Old-fashioned coal stoves, circa 1830. Though improvements were made, these stoves were still considered heavy even one hundred years later—a fact that seemed to have eluded our two "heroes." *Courtesy of the Library of Congress.*

They were taken to a youth detention facility to await trial in Children's Court. That was a sticky situation.

It should be standard procedure if you are going to steal clothing that you take the tags off, although I do love it when the criminals are as "bright" as Harold Frick. Frick was arrested in 1936 after a detective spotted the tag on his trousers and became suspicious. The pants were stolen from a North Salina Street store. Frick was awarded nine months in the county pen for his thievery. Fred Ferrence and Clarence Yeldon were arraigned for stealing three cartons of shoes valued at $350 from Stanton Express Company. I guess 1936 was national Steal Your Apparel year.

William Rennie was arrested in October 1898 after being charged with stealing pool balls from a number of poolrooms throughout the city. Detective Doolittle arrested Rennie as he was escorting another prisoner to jail. Rennie, a baker, claimed he was not responsible for the theft because his mind had not been clear for some time. There are several jokes in there somewhere that really should remain hidden. Rack 'em!

If you're going to make a fashion statement, it's probably best if you actually purchase the item you have your heart set on. William L. Carr took a liking to a fancy vest pattern he saw in Henry Bassler's store at 414 South Salina Street. Carr might have liked the vest pattern, but apparently the idea of actually paying for it didn't cross our stalwart's mind. He was arrested for petit larceny and convicted. He remained a guest of the county for four months courtesy of Justice Thompson. The vest probably didn't go with the striped prison pajamas.

A woodcut of prisoners at the state prison in Auburn, New York, circa 1840. *Courtesy of the Library of Congress.*

Davis Rothschild, sixteen, and Israel Abrams, fifteen, were cut to the quick when they were arrested for stealing three dozen pocketknives from Spaulding and Company on West Jefferson Street on October 21, 1898. Syracuse Police detective Doolittle arrested the pair when they attempted to sell the purloined pocketknives.

James Donnigan was no stranger to police court in December 1892. Donnigan admitted that he had been arrested over fifty times for drunkenness, and he couldn't explain why he had stolen a ham, stating that he lived in a boardinghouse and had no need for ham. Donnigan was apparently on the verge of *delirium tremens*. The judge sentenced him to forty days in the county penitentiary, commenting that while there he might get the medical care for his drunkenness.

It can be mind boggling to survey the things that a person will steal or why they'll steal them. We'll likely visit the lairs of thieves yet again. There are so many larcenous people and so little time.

Chapter 17

"CAN'T WE ALL JUST GET ALONG?": ASSAULT

Sometimes things get out of hand and words turn to fisticuffs. Many times, alcohol is involved, but sometimes, the person doing the thumping is just plain ornery. Husbands assault wives, and vice versa. Violence is never an answer in domestic disputes, and yet it is resorted to far too often even today.

June 12, 1865, must have been a rather exciting day in Syracuse's First Ward. Robert Stokes was arrested and fined twenty-five dollars for assault and battery against Mrs. Briggs. He was also fined an additional five dollars for assaulting her husband, Ambrose. Mary Welch was arrested for assaulting Catharine Rheddy and fined two dollars. Edward Rheddy was arrested for thumping Mary Welch and fined twelve dollars. Can't we all just get along?

Philonzo Spencer was convicted of assault with a deadly weapon on March 29, 1865. The jury recommended him to the mercy of the court. He was asked if he had anything to say and stated he did not. The court sentenced him to nine years and six months hard labor in Auburn Prison. Apparently, four years of war weren't enough for him.

Ewen Brittain apparently didn't like Thomas Kempster much. On September 22, 1853, Brittain was arrested by Officer Davis and charged with assault and battery against Kempster. What better way to celebrate the new autumn season than by thumping your fellow man? It seemed like a good idea to Nat Scott, Owen Brittain and Patrick Whalen, who were arrested by the resolute and busy Officer Davis and charged with assault and battery against John Van Buren on that same day. Scott settled and paid costs. The other two were released on bail.

Sometimes the person complaining would do well to shut up. Such is the case of George Wyatt, who in 1904 was, to quote the *Syracuse Post-Standard*, "a well-known character about town." Wyatt sued John J. Clark for assault and battery. Apparently, the seventy-year-old Wyatt wanted the door to his apartment house open. Clark, Wyatt's landlord, apparently wanted the door kept closed. During the disagreement, which took place May 1, 1903, Clark allegedly knocked down Wyatt, who could not get up without assistance. During the course of the trial, it was discovered that Wyatt had previously been arrested sixteen times for charges including intoxication and breach of peace, once on the complaint of his wife. Clark's lawyer effectively argued that Wyatt was quarrelsome, and Clark was exonerated.

Whatever happened to fists? Charles R. Augustin was charged with assaulting James Kemp in 1885. Kemp claimed that Augustin assaulted him with a loaded hose at 123 James Street and was asking for $1,000 in damages. In an era when boxing was considered a gentlemanly sport, smacking someone around with a hose modified into a sap just wasn't considered sporting. After all, this isn't professional wrestling!

There are those who will tell you that business can be rough. And historians will tell you that in the days before reform and regulations, anything went. Perhaps they were thinking about Charles E. Shattuck when they made that statement. Real estate can be a dog-eat-dog world, and it was certainly a rough-and-tumble profession in 1902, when Shattuck and Charles E. O'Donnell were in negotiations over Shattuck's purchase of the Hotel Almond on the corner of Almond and Madison Streets. O'Donnell went to Shattuck's office in the Kirk Block to demand payment due him relating to the Hotel Almond transaction. During the business meeting, Shattuck allegedly punched and tried to strangle O'Donnell. At the time of Shattuck's arraignment, court action was pending on the business dispute. This altercation brought new meaning to the phrase "turf war."

According to the August 24, 1905 issue of the *Syracuse Post-Standard*, George Doyle brought suit in municipal court for assault and battery against Patrolman John Savage. Doyle maintained that Savage assaulted him without provocation after demanding to know where Doyle was going. He also stated that it wasn't a case of mistaken identity, noting that the policeman threw him to the ground and "pounded" him. Savage's side of the story was not printed.

When you have the nickname "Slugger" and you're not in the news because of your athletic ability, it's probably an indication that you're likely going to be in trouble with the law at some point in your life. Such was the case of James

A boxer from the 1870s. While the "sweet science" remains popular, outside of the boxing ring, it's called assault. *Courtesy of the Library of Congress.*

"Slugger" Murphy, who was arrested on September 13, 1902, for assault in the third degree against his father. Murphy was well known to Syracuse police, having been arrested several times for intoxication and abusing his aged parents. Apparently, honoring Mom and Dad wasn't high on Slugger's lists of priorities.

We've all heard of ugly separations and divorces, but for Solomon Spector, it got really ugly. Spector's estranged wife sued him, alleging that he had assaulted her, and asked $1,000,000 in damages. She also had a previous suit for "adequate alimony" pending. The trial, which took place in September 1948, proves just how contentious marriage can be. The Spectors had been separated since 1946 and Solomon, an automobile dealer, was paying $65 a month in temporary alimony. Mr. Spector was countersuing to obtain an annulment. So much for "to have and to hold."

We have been told since we were children that violence never solves anything, but as the aforementioned stories show, that doesn't mean that people won't resort to it on occasion. When they do, they're liable to be arrested and ultimately serve time in the hoosegow.

Chapter 18

CRIMINAL COMBINES:
GANGS IN SYRACUSE

These days, when we think of gangs, the immediate image that comes to mind is the street gangs that plague urban America. Some will conjure up images of the gangs of the 1920s and figures like Al Capone and Bugs Moran in Chicago or the New York gangs that melded into what we now call organized crime. Indeed, from the birth of the nation, there has been some form of gang crime, from the Dead Rabbits and Whyos of New York City to the James and Younger gang of the Old West. Gangs have committed and abetted almost every crime imaginable in the pantheon of miscreant behavior. Syracuse has not been immune to this malady and probably will not be for the foreseeable future. Who were some of the notable gangs in Syracuse's past and how did they change the criminal face of the city? Shall we take a stroll?

To think of youthful gang activity as a recent phenomenon would be awe-inspiringly wrong. Nor was youth gang activity confined to major metropolitan areas. In February 1898, Syracuse police inspector O'Brien arrested a gang of youthful thieves for theft of a copper boiler. Tom Welch, Robert Welch, John Broderick, John Dunley and Jimmy Doyle were all apprehended. Robert Welch was the oldest member of the gang, whose ages ranged from eleven to sixteen. The gang met in a tumbledown building called the "hut." John Broderick, self-confessed leader of the gang, was only eleven years old at the time of his arraignment. According to the police, the gang was well organized and planned their robberies to take place in the hours after school let out. Broderick, who had an extensive history with the law, was sentenced to a term at the Saint Vincent Reformatory in Utica. The others were released to their parents with a stern warning from the court to not appear there again.

Another gang called themselves the Chain Gang, and perhaps that was fitting. Known by police in 1897 as the Daggett gang, they were wanted for a string of burglaries across the city. The gangsters were also notorious for cracking safes. After a sweeping series of arrests that nabbed thirteen of

the gang's members, three confessed to a variety of crimes and implicated others. In addition to the burglary charges, members of the gang were charged with assault and were suspected of the murder of Edward Connell in Dave Daggett's saloon. Among those charged was Peter Fitzgerald, who

Below: View from the Dead Rabbits barricade on Bayard Street at the height of the battle. This lithograph was based on an 1857 battle between the Dead Rabbits and the Bowery Boys, two notorious New York gangs of the 1850s.

pleaded guilty to four counts of burglary. The court delayed his sentencing until he could testify against others in the gang. Fitzgerald implicated John Harrington, who was under indictment for the murder of Edward Connell; Timothy Harrington; and Cornelius Fitzgerald, reputed to be the worst of the gang. Peter and Cornelius Fitzgerald (no relation) were sentenced to terms of five years and five years and eight months, respectively.

Though his activities never centered in Syracuse, gangster Arthur Flegenheimer, better known as Dutch Schultz, would spice up Syracuse newspapers in 1935, when the racketeer stood trial in Syracuse for tax evasion in April. Schultz's lawyers managed to get a change of venue from the city of New York, where they believed Arthur would not get a fair trial based on his reputation. While the police were not fond of Dutch, some of the city's luminaries found him affable and mild mannered. The racketeer even implied that he might make his home in Syracuse. Apparently, he impressed the federal jury in Syracuse, as he was found not guilty of the charges. Special prosecutor Thomas E. Dewey was tasked with bringing the New York rackets under control, and he did so with a vengeance. Schultz became preoccupied with killing Dewey, and the other members of organized crime's nascent board of directors decided that Dutch had to go. On October 23, 1935, six months after his trial in Syracuse, Charles Workman and Mendy Weiss murdered Schultz.

As Franklin D. Roosevelt prepared to enter the White House for the first of four terms, two men were threatened with jail. On January 12, 1933, bartenders William Ryan and William Callahan were offered the option of testifying about the liquor and beer rackets in Syracuse or being charged with contempt of court. Prosecutors wanted information on the gangs that robbed and wrecked an alleged speakeasy run by Buddy Carroll on East Washington Street and the bar on West Genesee and Fayette Streets the same night. The two bartenders were questioned in the grand jury room after a night in custody. The district attorney also interviewed several reputed gang leaders and bootleggers. The leader of the rumrunning gang in Solvay, a village just to the west of Syracuse, declined the district attorney's gracious invitation and headed south with several of his associates. The inquiries came in response to a war between rival bootlegging gangs. Police also arrested Earl Welch, Morris MacKinter and John Bradley, all of whom received bail. MacKinter also used the alias of Red Mack. It was believed at the time that the bar wreckers were part of "Owney" Madden's gang. Though Madden, who was based in New York City, was serving a prison term in Sing Sing, he still wielded considerable influence. Police believed the raid might have been in retaliation for the murder of Larry Fay, a Madden lieutenant who was gunned down by two Syracusans on New Years night. A total of nine establishments were wrecked in the gang war. By the standards of the brutal rampages of the New York gangs, including the English-born Madden's or Chicago gang wars, Syracuse got off rather easily. With the end of Prohibition, the beer gangs in Syracuse faded away or moved on to other ventures. Madden retired from gang life in 1935 when police scrutiny became too intense. He died in 1964 at the age of seventy-two.

Gangs still plague the Salt City, and it is certain that we will see them for the foreseeable future. But police continue to battle them, and strides are being made. It is doubtful that we will see gangs on a par with Dutch Schultz's or Al Capone's, but every gang in Syracuse threatens the city's tranquility. We can do without that aspect of the Roaring Twenties.

Chapter 19

MAKING MONEY THE OLD-FASHIONED WAY III:
SCHEMES, FRAUDS AND CON GAMES

There are people who are averse to the idea of actually working an honest job for their pay. It has been that way since man started building towns and cities, and it will continue until Gabriel plays a solo on his famous horn. These are the people who use their skills not to better themselves but to bilk their fellow man out of their hard-earned money. Con men and women prey on those who aspire to wealth and security. Notorious swindler Joseph "Yellow Kid" Weil claimed that he never cheated honest men, only rascals. Weil, reputed to be the greatest con man of the early twentieth century, said, "They wanted something for nothing—I gave them nothing for something." There is some truth to Weil's assertion even today. We've already talked politics, so let us venture instead to other realms.

Syracuse grew with the salt trade and the Erie Canal. As the city grew and prospered, the con men and swindlers migrated here, bringing with them con games and the desire to make wealth at the hands of the unwary. All too often, they were successful.

Sometimes the con man preys on those who would do them a good turn. On May 12, 1896, Polisto Guisso met two fellow Italians. Though strangers, the men convinced Guisso to hold a bag supposedly containing $7,000 for them. In return, they received $125 from the Madison Street resident. The two men then offered to pay Guisso $10 for holding the bag overnight for them. The duo claimed they had inherited the money from an uncle out west and were returning to Italy. They convinced Guisso to front them $125 so they could close out their affairs before sailing the next day. After withdrawing $100 from the bank, Guisso handed the money to the men, who promptly disappeared. The next day, when the pair had not returned, Guisso opened the bag to discover that the $7,000 was actually worthless scraps of paper. In a pattern that is all too familiar today, he waited a week before telling anyone that he had been scammed. Police detectives worked to discover the identities of the two con men but were unsuccessful.

Since the advent of the stock market, swindlers have found it easy to manipulate stocks and bilk people out of money. Typically, these self-titled financial gurus tell their victims they will garner untold riches and financial security, but usually, the results are a staggering loss of money that is rarely recovered. As the month of June 1899 came to a close, Charles W. Mix faced a battery of lawsuits alleging fraud. His two companies, Germania Land Company and the Realty and Investment Company, allegedly received over $18,000 in cash and real estate from residents of Syracuse's German section.[20] The residents received stocks that claimed to be "gilt-edged security." At the time, the district attorney stated that there were hundreds unaware that the purchased stock was worthless. The old adage was true then as well: If it sounds too good to be true, it probably is.

In April 1930, Stephen P. Toadvine of the Better Business Bureau advised people in Syracuse about several frauds perpetrated in the city and elsewhere that were making the rounds. The promise of vast wealth and land can impel people who are otherwise intelligent individuals to make some stupid choices. Several schemes were used in 1930 to help the gullible divest themselves of their money. The Drake Scheme floated the idea that the victim was an heir of the famous English seadog. The perpetrators collected several thousand dollars in expenses, claiming that these expenses were part of the ongoing attempt to secure the lost monies and land owed to the heirs. In another twist, three separate schemes akin to the aforementioned Drake scheme claimed to be holding title to the ground that Trinity Church stands on. One scheme, named after Aureke Jans Bogardus, whom Bogardus Corners[21] was named for, claimed to have found property belonging to the supposed heirs of Mr. Bogardus. The Emmerich Scheme was named after a partner of John Jacob Astor and purported to be holding the same land as the Bogardus claim. Two of the sponsors of the Emmerich Scheme were sentenced to lengthy prison terms. Finally, we come to the Robert Macomber scheme, which occurred during the same time as the Bogardus Scheme but went inactive due to a lack of success. Like the famed Peralta Land Grant Scheme,[22] all of these schemes promise vast riches in return for a "small" investment to cover expenses. These games were the precursor of today's Nigerian oil scams.

With all the uproar these days over what might happen to Medicare and how best to save it, we forget that medical insurance fraud has been with us since insurance first started being offered. The vast majority of doctors are honest, hard working and devoted to their patients. Then there is my next trio of miscreants. Doctors Edward J. Eckel, Albert A. Rubin and Israel Herman were convicted of insurance fraud in January 1935. Each doctor pleaded guilty to petit larceny and was sentenced to pay $200 or serve a day in jail for each dollar not paid. They were swept up in an investigation that netted fifty-eight people for insurance fraud. The fraud amounted to $100,000 in false claims made against the Employers Liability Insurance Company. The trio could have received a year in prison and a $500 fine.

In September 1934, two women pleaded guilty to petit larceny. Ethel M. Dunn and Irene Woldridge were arraigned on grand larceny charges after being arrested for filing a fake automobile accident claim against the Lumberman's Mutual Casualty Company of Illinois for $870. The two women were fined $100 and granted probation. I'll wager that the stunt played Hell with the insurance rates.

In a variation of the scam played on Polisto Guisso, a pair of women liberated Mrs. Nina Crumb of $1,600. The scam, which took place July 26, 1949, involved the usual promised large sum of money for a small investment. When Mrs. Crumb went to the lawyer's office indicated by the two scammers, the lawyer had no knowledge of any of the money Mrs. Crumb mentioned. Mrs. Crumb, realizing she had been duped, contacted Syracuse police.

There are still scammers and con men with us today. Computers play a large part in their efforts, and I wonder what Joseph Weil would make of that. The lost purse gag and the Drake heirs scam are really not much different than the Nigerian oil-money scam. The major difference is that now the fraud can be committed from a laptop in the comfort of the thief's hotel room.

Chapter 20

VANDALISM FOR FUN AND MAYBE PROFIT

Sometimes you just have to indulge those destructive urges that seem like a really great idea at the time. Of course, my mother would have told me that indulging those urges wasn't a good idea. We think of vandalism as a juvenile problem, and sometimes, it is. But we've already seen several instances that prove otherwise. When we think of vandalism, we tend to see a kid with a can of spray paint tagging a building wall or stop sign. In fact, the word comes from the Vandals, nomadic raiders who sacked Rome in an orgy of destruction so stunning that their name lives on. Syracuse has not seen that sort of destruction, but the modern version is bad enough.

On the night of December 1, 1893, would-be lumberjacks cut down two trees in front of the houses of John Kurtz and Jacob Kurtz on Lock Street. The Kurtz brothers reported the vandalism to police the morning of December 2. That seems like a lot of work for a practical joke, Paul Bunyan!

In August 1897, the Onondaga County Savings Bank building was brand new. The Renaissance Revival–style building was one of the first steel-frame buildings in the city. The owners were justifiably proud and enjoyed letting the public view the opulent interior from the observation area on the roof of the building. During the first week of August, vandals defaced the walls of the bank building. Long gouges were rudely chipped into the masonry walls. Crude caricatures and what the August 6, 1897 *Syracuse Evening Herald* called "autographs" defaced the walls. Bank officials closed the observation area in response to the vandalism.

Two years earlier, on June 11, 1895, burglars had broken into Saint Peter's German Evangelical Lutheran Church. Not content with stealing the contents of the missionary box, they broke furniture and fixtures in the church as well. The miscreants were not caught.

It's not unusual to hear of vandalism on Halloween, and over the years, it has come to be expected. The occasional assault on someone's house with eggs or the papering of their shrubbery with toilet paper seems at times to be a rite of passage. A few hours of quality time with a garbage bag or a bucket of soapy water and clean rags usually suffices to remove the signs of the night's debauchery. In that, I guess kids weren't much different in 1922

Halloween and the Minnesota Snowball. This pen-and-ink drawing by Charles Lewis Bartholomew conveys the impending winter in Minnesota, but winter follows Halloween just as quickly in Syracuse. The holiday remains a prime time for minor acts of vandalism. *Courtesy of the Library of Congress.*

than they are today. But some of the Halloween revelers not content with smashing pumpkins or papering greenery got a bit more ambitious.

While bonfires have long been part of Samhain[23] celebrations in ancient Ireland, the ancient Celts didn't steal other people's lumber carts to make them. In 1923, vandals stole a lumber cart from its parking place on Manlius Street and pushed it into the intersection of James Street and Teall Avenue. They set the cart on fire and added some stray realty signs to help fuel the impromptu blaze. In addition, a number of windows were smashed in both cars and storefronts, including that of the Letterman Company. The modern Halloween pastime of soaping windshields was not neglected that night. The capstone of the evening was the parking of an engineless Ford and its occupant on the north side's most precarious precipice. We don't know just how drunk the owner of the car was. The flivver had been parked in a garage on Butternut Street while undergoing repairs. The owner had been part of the unplanned celebration. No more pumpkin juice for him!

Two years later, in a case disturbing for its bigoted tone, Herbert R. Johns stood in front of Judge Barnum accused of vandalism. The Craddock Street resident had painted "KKK" on the front of Holy Rosary Roman Catholic Church on Halloween night. Father Mahon, the parish priest, asked the court to show leniency to Johns, adding that he didn't believe the vandalism was malicious. Herbert R. Johns was freed thanks to Father Mahon's intercession. He could have been sentenced to seven years in prison. The judge admonished Johns, stating that his act could have stirred up religious hatred. Johns's fiancée was present at the February 27, 1925 sentencing. She must have been so proud!

Seven years later, in an attempt to stem the annual spate of vandalism, Police Chief Martin Cadin ordered his police officers to arrest any boys caught vandalizing property. Cadin's decree came after a flood of complaints ranging from damaged shrubbery to broken car windows and deflated tires had come into the Syracuse Police Department. Though Halloween had been a time for pranks for several decades, the mischief was beginning to start earlier each year. By 1932, the Halloween pranks were beginning in the first week of October and becoming more and more destructive.

In what they claimed was a prank, nine youths were arraigned for vandalism on July 18, 1946. The boys did $350 worth of damage to Lincoln Park. Several teeter-totters were damaged and thrown into the pool. A chute was ripped up and thrown in the same pool, the railing around the pool was removed and a teeter-totter was used to break down a door to the field house. Four of the boys, all of whom were over sixteen, admitted their guilt. A fifth youth pleaded not guilty. Children's Court held four other youths under the age of sixteen for disposal. Judge Homer Walsh ordered the youths to pay the $350 in damages. They couldn't blame it on Halloween this time.

Sometimes you just have to wonder where Mommy and Daddy were. On April 3, 1950, police arrested three juveniles, aged seven, nine and ten, for vandalism. The trio of youthful offenders had broken into the Reddin Iron Works on Marcellus Street and did damage so extensive to the factory that all but four of the fifty-two employees were sent home while repairs were being made. The children broke windows, spilled a twenty-gallon barrel of germicide, damaged clothing belonging to workers and destroyed several machines. Police officials stated that it was the most extensive vandalism they had seen in some time. The miscreants confessed after being taken to headquarters.

Obviously, vandalism is still with us, and no one solution will totally eradicate it. My father's specific cure, had I been involved in any of the abovementioned incidents, would have been to heat up my tail feathers, and I would have been working to pay the damages. Perhaps community service to work off the costs of repairing the skullduggery will cure a huge portion of this particular problem.

Chapter 21

NO JOY IN THIS RIDE: VEHICLE THEFT

I magine stepping into a sun-filled day after a much-needed shopping adventure only to find your vehicle gone. You know you didn't park in a handicap spot or in front of a fire hydrant. An explicative rises to your lips as you realize that someone has stolen your car. This crime happens every day in cities and towns all across America. You would be forgiven for thinking it is a modern problem. Alas, vehicle theft has been with us since man put wheels on things and started riding around in them. It happens everywhere, and Syracuse is no exception.

We don't think of firemen as criminals, and thankfully, most of them are not. A dispute regarding the ownership of a horse arose in February 1911 after horseman James Kanaley of Syracuse Fire Department Engine Company One led a horse away from Harry Flesher's stable. Flesher alleged that Kanaley had offered to buy the horse before leading it away and refusing to return the horse or pay for it. Kanaley countered that the horse was his and that he had loaned it to a cart man who was interested in buying the animal. Kanaley was paroled awaiting trial.

What a dutiful son! On November 15, 1905, Charles E. Pennoyer was convicted of stealing a horse and wagon from his mother. The aged and crippled Mrs. Pennoyer was present throughout the proceedings. The nineteen-year-old Pennoyer had also stolen money from his mother and schoolteacher and made off with a ring belonging to his sister. Mrs. Pennoyer had lent the wagon to Mrs. Francis Green of Fabius. Charles took the wagon from there and sold it.

A 1909 Stanley Steamer at the Wells Automobile Museum in Wells, Maine. Even that early, cars were being stolen. *Courtesy of Peggy Reilly.*

Fourteen years later, on November 14, 1919, Charles Kinsalla and Michael Staff were sentenced to serve a term at the State Industrial School in Rochester after the youths stole an automobile belonging to William J. Caruthers of Emma Street. Though he was tempted to show the boys leniency, Justice Shove sentenced the boys to set an example for other would-be car thieves. Justice Shove said automobile theft was "almost epidemic" at the time.

Since the advent of the automobile, car theft has been a headache for police and big business for criminals. On December 5, 1927, Buffalo, New York police called Syracuse the hub of a statewide auto theft ring. Buffalo detectives surmised that thirty cars had been stolen in November of that year, of which twenty were possibly sold in Syracuse. Four years earlier, in April 1923, Frederick Hoffmann was indicted for heading a gang of car thieves in the Syracuse area. The youth was charged with two counts of grand larceny. George Maney and Ivan Tillinghast were indicted along with Hoffmann.

If you're going to be a successful car thief, it helps to not be seen driving the automobile you stole by the owner. Eighteen-year-old William Wenzel stole a car belonging to Frank Janowski while Mr. Janowski was in church on January 4, 1931. As Wenzel was driving away, Janowski spotted him and gave chase in another car. Wenzel was quickly arrested, arraigned and found guilty of stealing the car.

Taxi drivers can be a competitive lot. Such was the case when a rate war led to two cabbies being arrested in January 1933. The rate war between Yellow Cab and ABC Taxi escalated to the point where a cab was stolen and wrecked. William Harrington was arrested for second-degree grand larceny. The ABC cabby allegedly stole the taxi after Yellow Cab forced a rate cut on rival cab companies. The theft was followed by a wild police chase through the city and the destruction of the cab. Seymour Townsend, another ABC driver, was held as a material witness, and police expected to make more arrests as the investigation progressed. The theft prompted the Syracuse Common Council to table plans to push through the rate cuts demanded by Yellow Cab.

Mom and Dad must have been so proud! Paul Klock was arrested November 15, 1936, after two Syracuse policemen caught him breaking into a car on Forest Hill Drive. The eighteen-year-old was arraigned for the alleged car theft and held for disposition by the grand jury in January 1937. Klock waived examination in police court.

Two youths, Leon W. Millius and Joseph R. Swidowski, were convicted of committing a series of burglaries and car thefts in 1938. The pair was sentenced on May 17. Millius was awarded two years in Auburn Prison, while Swidowski garnered an indeterminate stay at Elmira Reformatory. May 1938 must have been car-theft month in Syracuse, as Floyd R. Fuller, a resident of South State Street in Syracuse, was also convicted of grand larceny for stealing a car. He was sentenced to five to ten years in connection with the automobile theft. Bus fare couldn't have been that bad in 1938!

Sometimes, I guess it depends on who the judge is. Stephen D. Von Hoody, George P. Chimber and Charles H. Eckhard were convicted of grand theft auto in May 1946. The trio were given five years probation for their little joy rides. These guys got lucky!

Charles R. Smith of Bridgeton, New Jersey, seriously needed a hobby. On June 20, 1948, Smith was arrested at Joseph McVann's diner on South Franklin Street and charged with third-degree burglary and auto theft. Smith attempted to break into the diner but was thwarted by Mr. McVann. He then stole a car on South Avenue and returned to break into the diner again but was captured when McVann threatened the would-be burglar with a nonexistent pistol. There are times when the usually sound advice of "If at first you don't succeed, try, try again" should be ignored. This was one of them.

Apparently, there were not enough cars to steal in Youngstown, Ohio. Twenty-three-year-old James Stewart pleaded guilty to first-degree grand larceny on December 6, 1950, after being arrested for stealing a 1948 sedan from a parking lot on East Fayette Street in Syracuse. Judge Leo Breed ordered Stewart held for sentencing.

Vehicle theft continues to be a problem in the Salt City, though with better policing techniques and theft deterrence systems, it may not be the problem it once was. These days, the opportunistic car thief is looking for unlocked cars. And although locking the car won't necessarily stop car thieves, it will hopefully send them on to greener pastures.

Chapter 22

ROLL THEM BONES:
GAMBLING IN THE SALT CITY

Today, with casinos springing up all over the place and millions of people playing the lottery in hopes of that one big score that will put them on "Easy Street," it can be hard to remember that it wasn't terribly long ago that gambling was illegal in Syracuse and New York State. As you'll remember, one of the Prohibition cases I detailed in an earlier chapter began as a gambling raid. It has been said that there is no such thing as easy money, but that doesn't stop the gullible or lazy from trying to find it.

Monday, April 27, 1857, was a busy day for Justice Thompson, who was presiding over a police court packed to the gills. Frank Willet, Dennis Donigan and James Welch were arrested for gambling. Justice Thompson fined each man two dollars. Michael McAvoy stood in front of Thompson charged with pitching pennies on the Sabbath. His transgression cost him two dollars as well. Finally, Joseph Orange was arrested by Officer Walsh and charged with keeping a gambling house. He was fined twenty-five dollars.

Twenty-five years later, the December 30, 1882 *Syracuse Standard* castigated Chief of Police Wright over his inability to close down several gaming houses in the immediate downtown area. The newspaper's crusade began after a farmer who lost sixteen dollars and other victims of the mountebanks related their stories to the paper. For his part, Wright retorted that he and his men were carefully policing the area but that evidence of illegal gambling was proving elusive. The *Standard* alleged that gamblers were plying their trade brazenly in total disregard for the law. Through the latter half of the nineteenth century and the earlier decades of the twentieth century, civic leaders and clergymen railed against the evils of gambling and those who were less than enthusiastic in their prosecution of that particular vice in the Salt City. Ministers thundered fire-and-brimstone sermons condemning gaming and gamblers to the fiery depths of Gahanna. Temperance advocates like the Anti Saloon League and the Women's Christian Temperance Union joined them. Newspapers in Syracuse took up the clarion call with alacrity.

We expect politicians to be sore losers. Something in the nature of the political animal makes gracious acquiescing defeat in any venue odious. But we don't expect them to be sore winners. It was Michael W. Kelly's misfortune to lose a game of freeze out on November 15, 1888, to Alderman John D. Scanlon of the Tenth Ward. Kelly admitted he was gambling with the alderman but denied that he kept a gambling house. Scanlon and Kelly had been drinking together when the game ensued. After the game, Scanlon swore out a warrant against Kelly. Lawyers for both men tried unsuccessfully to get them to resolve the manner outside of the courtroom. Scanlon refused and told Kelly that he would produce other charges if Kelly tried to "crawl out"[24] from the gambling charge. Kelly then admitted to buying the alderman drinks as part of a challenge to Scanlon to do his worst. He added that he was under the influence of drink while they were playing, and he didn't believe Scanlon won the $200. He admitted to the court that he agreed to give Scanlon a check for the money, but the safe was closed. Justice Mulholland dismissed the men with the admonition that the assault case he was trying took precedence.

If I drive a few miles into Madison County, I can legally place a bet on a horse race. New York legalized off-track betting some years ago. In 1901, however, horse poolrooms, as off-track betting parlors were known then, were illegal. It certainly didn't help the district attorney's blood pressure when one was operating directly across the canal from the county courthouse. A bitter battle was being waged over racetrack gambling in the New York State legislature, and then as now, district attorneys had one eye on the law and one on their political aspirations. District Attorney Kline was no exception. In May 1901, Kline ordered Sheriff Marvin to close the offending establishment. The sheriff demanded a written order and received it. The raid, if it can be called that, was carried out, but no one was arrested, and none of the gambling paraphernalia was seized. The raid also did nothing to deter other gambling houses in the area. The public safety commissioner denied that there was any gambling going on in the city even after being told that the sheriff had raided the Water Street poolroom. I'll bet the DA was not amused.

A den on Baxter Street as pictured in a woodcut lithograph taken from *Frank Leslie's Illustrated Newspaper*, circa 1867. Dens like this flourished in Syracuse. *Courtesy of the Library of Congress.*

If you're going to get busted for gambling, could you at least find a game with a respectable pot? Syracuse police raided a gambling den on South Townsend Street on January 15, 1934, and upon arrival found three men playing a penny ante game called Pitty-Pat. After one of the players threw in a two-cent ante, Detectives Elijah Black and Edward Dolphin and acting detective Patrick Walsh arrested the trio. The night's biggest loser lost a whopping four cents and lamented being "dead broke." Otis Matlock was charged with running a gambling house, while Andrew Nugent and Ward Williams were arrested for being inmates of a gambling house. The raid was part of larger concerted effort to find and close gambling establishments in the South Townsend Street area.

On September 1, 1934, Syracuse police launched a major raid against slot machine owners in the city. Seventeen people were arrested for violating gambling laws. The one-armed bandits were located in several stores. Captain Blanchard of the Syracuse Police surreptitiously got his team into the stores and quickly executed the warrants. Twelve of the people arrested were charged with possessing gaming devices. The other five were charged with installing the slot machines. The raid was accomplished in under six hours. For the police, the raid was an unqualified success, but gambling would continue in the Salt City.

Thirteen years later, on Saint Patrick's Day, police acting on a phone tip raided a storeroom on East Castle Street. Frank Woolridge was nabbed for having five gambling machines. Woolridge claimed that the obsolete machines were for novelty purposes and had not been used for some time. The raid came on the heels of a grand jury investigation regarding missing slot machines. Deputy Sheriff Howard Mosher, a special investigator for the district attorney's office, arrested Anthony Sanfilippo, charging him with possession of lottery tickets. Sanfilippo's arrest came on the heels of a March 16, 1950 raid that netted Samuel Lloyd for gambling and selling liquor and beer without a license. Lloyd pleaded guilty to the charges. With all that excitement, who needs a Saint Patrick's Day parade?

A police vice squad raided the Idyll Hour restaurant on West Onondaga Street on May 6, 1950. Two men were arrested for accepting bets on the Kentucky Derby and other horse races. Detective Robert Holland placed Edward G. Fecca and George Tucci under arrest after police entered the restaurant and found customers placing bets on horse races. Holland stated that the recently opened restaurant had likely been taking baseball parleys for a few months. The gambling room was located in the rear of the restaurant.

Today, New York is home to several casinos run by Native American nations, the lottery is a fact of life and as I stated earlier, the state has also sanctioned off-track betting parlors. There are also chapters of Gamblers Anonymous active in the Syracuse area. But some forms of gambling are still illegal, and on any given night, you can find someone running a football or baseball pool if you know where to look. Like it or not, gambling is still a fixture of life in the Salt City.

Chapter 23

HELL NO, I WON'T GO:
DRAFT DODGERS AND BOUNTY JUMPERS

The days are long gone when the government paid bounties for people to enlist in the army. In point of fact, that was a system unique to the Civil War. The draft has been dormant since the end of the Vietnam War, though the machinery remains in place. We don't generally think of draft dodgers as criminals, but in fact, that is exactly what they were. The picture today is, depending on whom you ask, either a deluded leftist-leaning youth or that of a misunderstood hero.

The first draft[25] in the United States was signed into law in 1863 and worked, as later drafts did, on a lottery system. If your number came up, you had to go. The states actually offered bounties in a bid to meet their quotas during the Civil War. Very quickly, the unscrupulous found ways to take advantage of the flawed system. Bounty jumpers were one of the problems faced by civil and military authorities during the Civil War and its incarnation of the draft. The rich were afforded the options of buying out of one draft lottery for $100 or hiring a substitute. Newspapers from the time are crammed with advertisements offering bounties and men looking to hire substitutes to take their place in the army. In fact, the Syracuse Union Volunteer and Substitute Agency made a tidy sum offering foreign substitutes for drafted men who could afford their services.

One of the many caught up in the problematic draft system of the Civil War was student Owen Donovan. The incident transpired on Saturday March 11, 1865, when Mr. Donovan was arrested on the word of a Utica bounty broker and a vagabond who testified that Donovan was enlisted.

Several witnesses, including Donovan's uncle, James McGurk, testified that Mr. Donovan was a student and had been for over six months, and the Utica recruiting agent testified that Donovan had never enlisted. The young man spent a day and night in the jail cells of the county courthouse. There was money to be made in producing bodies for the army. Donovan was one of the first to be caught up, although briefly, in a flawed system that allowed the rich to buy their way out of the draft and others to get rich by means that were less than ethical.

The popular notion of the "Greatest Generation" is that they stepped up to the plate and did their job without complaint, joining the service and fighting until the war was over. For the most part, that is an accurate assessment. But there were also people like Merrill Lester of Gifford Street. Mr. Lester was arrested on December 12, 1944, and indicted for failure to report for induction and failure to notify his draft board that his address had changed. He was arraigned in May 1946 and tried in June of that year. He was sentenced to a year to two years at Walkill Prison and fined $500 for abandonment on the draft evasion charges.

What's in a name? William Downing believed that changing his name to Albert Downs would help him elude federal prison on draft evasion charges. It might have worked if Downing had stayed on the straight and narrow. The thirty-two-year-old convict was arrested in Cincinnati, Ohio, on New Years Eve 1947 for issuing false checks. When fingerprint experts ran his prints, they discovered that he was wanted on two separate federal charges. He was promptly turned over to federal authorities. Happy New Year, Mr. Downing!

Seven months earlier, Andrew J. Morabito was sentenced to four years in prison after pleading guilty to car theft and draft evasion charges. The East Laurel Street resident initially denied wrongdoing when arrested in Chicago. Morabito had been on the lam for several years prior to his April 1946 arrest. He was on probation when he disappeared on Halloween in 1941. He served his sentence in the federal prison in Atlanta, Georgia.

Syracuse, in the period between the Civil War and the start of the Korean War, saw very few draft dodgers and only one alleged bounty jumper. Perhaps it was a different time, or perhaps people had a different frame of mind. In 1972, Congress did away with the draft, but young men still have to register when they turn eighteen. For the last forty years, the nation has not needed to draft our young men to fight in the far-flung corners of the world. Hopefully this spells the end of people going to prison for evading the draft. Only time will tell.

Chapter 24

RAPE

R ape is a horrifying crime and one that no person should ever suffer. Rape is also one of the most underreported and misunderstood crimes faced by society. It is not a modern phenomenon. Society has been plagued with rape since the beginning of time. Experts suggest that rape is about power and dominance, and perhaps they are right. Still, it is a crime that is heinous in execution and scandalous in the way it is sometimes handled by authorities and society in general. The crime was rare enough in March 1859 that Syracuse's *Central City Courier* newspaper carried a report of a rape trial in Holyoke, Massachusetts. Unfortunately, that trend would not continue.

On April 30, 1857, Robert Sullivan was convicted of raping Ellen Desmond, who leapt from a fourth-story window and died as a result of the rape. Sullivan drew a life sentence in Auburn Prison, while James White, an alleged accomplice of Sullivan's, was acquitted on May 9, 1857.

The disappearance of a child is a parent's worst nightmare. In 1886, fourteen-year-old Mary Sullivan was enticed from her house by Henry and Mary Elizabeth Winchell. The Winchells took the girl to Rochester, where they forced her to marry Charles Hoyt. The Winchells were eventually arrested in Detroit. Henry Winchell was charged with kidnapping and rape, while his wife was charged with abduction. Mary Sullivan was promptly returned to her family.

On May 27, 1890, Mrs. L. Birdie Gemmell was assaulted and raped in her home while her husband was at work. The alleged suspect was her stepfather, Louis Bishop. According to Mrs. Gemmell, Bishop arrived with a package and asked for a cup of tea. She refused to take the package but offered to make him some coffee. As she climbed the stairs to make the coffee, Bishop seized her and rendered her unconscious. When the eighteen-year-old woman awoke, the suspect was gone. He was arrested the next day at the Rock Spring Brewery, where he was employed as a driver.

On November 19, 1902, William Smith was sentenced to ten years in Auburn Prison for raping Mrs. Anna Nugent. In addressing the court, Smith maintained his innocence and stated that he would serve the sentence as "an American citizen and soldier." He then thanked his lawyer and wished him luck. For his part, Judge Eggleston told the prisoner he would get three years and six months commuted from his sentence if he maintained good behavior. The courts found Smith guilty, but was he? I consider it one of those enigmas that sometimes plague our justice system. Given the advances in criminal forensics these days, I suspect that Smith would have been exonerated.

Louis D. Brookins paid the ultimate penalty for his crimes. The twenty-two-year-old Syracusan was executed at Ossining Prison on September 12, 1946, for the rape and strangulation of a Rochester hairdresser.

Anthony Bovee was arrested for raping a woman on West Colvin Street. The alleged rape took place July 26, 1948. According to the victim, Bovee offered to take her to meet her fiancé but instead attempted to attack her. She fled her attacker but was dragged back to the car and assaulted. She attempted to defend herself with a pocket mirror and a nail file. Due to a previous conviction, Bovee was held without bail.

Leonard Arnold Weston, also known as William J. Wheeler, was arraigned on May 21, 1950, for first-degree rape. The case involved the assault of a Southside woman. Justice Bamerick ordered the Gifford Street resident held without bail in order to give him time to find a lawyer. Weston's sentencing on an unlawful entry charge was postponed as well.

In an ideal world, parents nurture and protect their children, but sometimes, that parenting is noticeably absent. The Varney/Morgan case shook Syracuse in the early months of 1950. Mrs. Mary Varney and her eldest daughter, Mary Varney Morgan, were charged with preventing Mrs. Varney's fourteen-year-old daughter from testifying at a grand jury inquest looking into charges that Stephen Morgan, Mary Morgan's husband and the young girl's brother-in-law, had raped the fourteen-year-old. Mrs. Varney tried to have the girl spirited to Massachusetts to prevent her testifying for the grand jury. Stephen Morgan pleaded

The third Onondaga County Courthouse. *Courtesy of the Library of Congress.*

guilty to a reduced charge of assault. Mrs. Varney was sentenced to a year in the county penitentiary and was told she would be returned to answer further charges when her sentence was complete. Mrs. Morgan was sentenced to the woman's correctional facility at Bedford Hills and stripped of her probation that she was serving for being a wayward girl. The younger daughter was placed in a foster home.

Rape continues to plague the Salt City. Forensic techniques have improved, and with the now-common use of DNA, more convictions are being obtained against the actual culprits. Violent crimes such as rape are on the decline, but vigilant and prompt enforcement will be the key in perpetuating the downward trend.

Chapter 25

THE WEIRD AND UNUSUAL:
"YOU STOLE WHAT?"

Sometimes we have to revisit areas previously trodden. Perhaps we missed something the first time, or perhaps it's a guilty pleasure—like watching reruns of *Gilligan's Island* or *Dallas*. We've all done it even if we won't admit it to our friends. Thievery of the bizarre is a point in case. Sometimes you just have to ask why.

On February 9, 1865, unknown thieves entered the Putnam School on the corner of Jefferson and Montgomery Streets and stole two shawls belonging to students. The thieves pawned the shawls for a pittance. Officer Kelly tracked the missing shawls to the pawnshop in question and retrieved them. They were returned to the student owners, who could ill-afford to lose them.

I admire ambition. Six years earlier, on January 5, 1859, Peter Schug was arrested for theft, suspected of stealing $18.00 from Henry Herman's meat market. Schug resolutely denied the charge. Upon searching Schug, the missing money was found sewn into the waistband of his trousers. Jewelry belonging to Willard and Hawley Jewelers valued at $18.75 was also found in his possession. Officer Walsh arrested Schug for the theft. Schug subsequently confessed to the jewelry theft. $36.75 doesn't seem like a lot today, but back then it was three months wages for an army private.

If you're going to try to talk your way out of a theft charge, at least try to come up with an original and plausible story! Michele Guerimo was sentenced to four months in the Jamesville Penitentiary on December 13, 1898, for stealing a sample case from a Bentley and Settle's salesman. In his defense, Guerimo claimed someone asked him to hold the case for him and then never returned. The story failed to impress the justice, who advised Guerimo that if he didn't leave Syracuse, he would get another two-months stay in Jamesville. Guerimo promised he would leave when he got out.

I guess good seats are hard to find. Frank Bussey, a resident of 118 East Newell Street, was arrested on August 27, 1898, for stealing a bench from Henry F. Lawrence's barn in East Syracuse. His trial was held August 31, 1898. I'll guarantee he had a very good perch for the trial.

Gee, I thought whiskers were in style in 1899! At the turn of the century, Ernest Howe was arraigned for public intoxication. He was also charged with stealing a razor from Henry Bennett's Burnet Avenue shop. Howe denied the theft, but Justice Thomson didn't believe him. Howe pleaded to have the sentence suspended so he would not lose his job at the electric light works. I wonder how he liked the prison haircut?

The night of June 7, 1902, was a busy one for Syracuse police. In a period of four hours, five bicycles were stolen in the city, including one belonging to Mrs. Samuel Hawking of Montgomery Street. Mrs. Hawking's bicycle was recovered within fifteen minutes. George Smith was arrested for the crime when he was found in possession of the bicycle.

And I thought I was a voracious reader. Carmelo Romano was sentenced on July 23, 1908, to twenty-five days in the county pen for stealing eight

Motorized bicycles in the Wells Automobile Museum from the early 1900s. The bicycle on the right is a later variant with a motor wheel from 1909. *Courtesy of Peggy Reilly.*

hundred *Post-Standard* newspapers. The papers were left on the sidewalk near James and Warren Streets. Roman claimed that he thought they were old papers, but this was disproved when papers from doorways were also found in his cart. The theft was the largest in several years, accounting for about twenty-five dollars in newspapers.

Sometimes you just have to have a Baby Ruth. John Stone and Edward Bennett were sentenced to ten months in the county lockup for stealing candy from a railroad freight car. The sentencing took place October 29, 1920. Trick or treating would have been easier, guys.

On the night of August 17, 1923, burglars broke into John J. Connors café on North Salina Street. The miscreants made off with $19.75 in cash, a roll of pennies, three hundred cigarettes and several cigars. They forced a side door open to affect the theft. Café workers discovered the theft the next morning. That same day, a thief made off with a $50 box of adhesive tape from a delivery truck parked in Bank Alley.

They say the apple doesn't fall far from the tree, and in the case of fifteen-year-old Joseph Rospendowski, this is especially true. Rospendowski was arrested on October 28, 1922, after being charged with stealing a lap robe from a car parked in Washington Square. Joseph's arrest followed quickly on the heels of his father's arraignment for murdering Peter Sokolowski. Walter Rospendowski had been indicted the day before.

Other people's lager—the beer to have when you're having much more than one! On October 4, 1945, thieves stole between seventy-five and one hundred cases of beer from a freight car on a siding at the Cayuga Beverage Company on Spencer Street. Glenn Canfield, an employee of the company, discovered the theft when he reported to work the morning of October 5, 1945 and promptly reported the theft to police.

Benjamin Franklin gave us the following sage advice: "Early to bed, early to rise makes a man healthy, wealthy and wise." But I'm not sure he had Mrs. Helen Swansbrough in mind. On September 21, 1949, Mrs. Swansbrough reported that her South State Street home had been broken into and an alarm clock stolen. She did not estimate the value of the purloined timepiece. Time flies indeed!

That wasn't what they meant by "the golden years," gramps! A ninety-year-old man was arrested for petit larceny on September 1, 1950, after he stole $1.80 in merchandise from the F.W. Woolworth Co. department store at 301 South Salina Street in downtown Syracuse. The old gent was released into the custody of his sixty-nine-year-old son after officials at the store withdrew the shoplifting complaint. His son must have been so proud!

You never know when you'll need a polishing rag! The May 21,1940 issue of the *Syracuse Herald Journal* described the "pushcart brigade" as a brigade of youths that systematically looted N. Ullman and Sons junk shop on Madison Street of over two tons of rags. Apparently, the neighbors didn't think the act was unusual. What kind of neighborhood was the 300 block of Madison Street in 1940? That same night, thieves stole two pinball machines from the Gravity gas station at 2707 South Salina Street. May 20 was a busy night for the police. A week later three boys were arrested for stealing six bottles of soda pop from a gas station at the corner of North Geddes Street and West Genesee Street. Clifton Moody, William E. Jackson and Clyde E. Branch pleaded guilty to petit larceny and were held for sentencing. They must have been thirsty.

We accumulate a lot of things as we traverse through life. As long as we continue to accumulate, there are those who will want what we have and will lack the desire to pay for the items or work for them. In that, the Salt City is no different than anywhere else.

Chapter 26

CIVIL UNREST:

OTHER RIOTS IN THE SALT CITY

I come from a generation that saw news of riots on the television and in the newspapers as a seemingly daily occurrence. Growing up in the 1960s after President Kennedy was assassinated, it appeared that everyone was angry. We don't think of the preceding years as filled with civil unrest. Yet, they had their fair share of riots. Some were fueled by racial or ethnic bigotry, much like the Cook Coffee House riot was. Others were the result of perceived wrongs by big business or government. Syracuse has seen very few riots in its history, and compared to the massive New York City draft riots of 1863 or the Haymarket Riot of Chicago, they might be seen as mere flashes in the pan. But Syracuse is no Chicago, and what may seem like an out-of-hand block party in the Windy City is a big deal in the Salt City.

On August 12, 1898, ethnicity and conflicting tasks led to a brawl between workmen for the Syracuse Rapid Transit Railway Company and Italian workmen hired to move a sewer derrick. The fracas started when the derrick crew wanted to cross tracks that the railway workers were engaged in repairing. When the Italians tried to move the derrick, the railway workers protested and attempted to remove the derrick by force. The derrick crew resisted, but the railway workers outnumbered them. They retreated and gathered reinforcements. The fight degenerated into a rock-throwing melee. The railway foreman, Mr. Davis, suffered several gashes and was assisted to a pharmacy. Four members of the derrick crew—Antonio Michilia, Giovanni Christiani, Antonio Modena and Frank Sposato—were arrested. Just as the Cook Coffee House riot was fueled by ethnic bigotry, so too was the derrick

The Riots at New York. This lithograph was featured in *Harper's Weekly Magazine* in the aftermath of New York City's draft riots in 1863. Syracuse's riots were tame by comparison. *Courtesy of the Library of Congress.*

riot that blocked North Salina Street. Today, the reporter using the ethnic slur printed in the newspaper account would likely find himself on the street. But at the height of the Gilded Age, it was "journalism at its finest."

Perhaps they didn't like the show. On February 24, 1908, three Syracuse University students were arrested and charged with breach of the peace and four others detained for questioning after rioting broke out in the Weiting Opera House. Charles F. Henry, Arthur Muir and Linus Cave were held for participating in the February 21 riot. Police expected to make more arrests in the case. I don't remember Riots 101 being a course when I was in college.

Call it a university rivalry or "boys will be boys" if you like, but the Syracuse police called it a riot. The February 26, 1925 fracas started when Syracuse University sophomores tried to break up a dinner of College of Forestry freshmen being held in the chamber of commerce building. The fight escalated to the point where over a dozen chemical stink bombs were thrown and the interior of the chamber of commerce dining room was in danger of ruination. The sophomore contingent gained access to the building by climbing fire escapes after the freshmen locked the doors. A window was broken and a door smashed. The dining room was unusable the next day because of the stink bombs. Chamber of commerce officials refused to press charges. I don't think that was the kind of education their parents were paying for.

When labor strife comes to Syracuse, it's usually in the form of a strike in which catcalls might be exchanged between strikers and plant managers. Rarely does the specter of violence rear its head. Thursday, August 20, 1937, was the exception to the rule. On that day, a force of two hundred to three hundred strikers attacked hundreds of workers at the Remington-Rand typewriter factory on Gifford Street. The riot stemmed from a contentious labor dispute marked by a strike at Precision Tools in Elmira, a subsidiary of Rand, and ongoing court battles between the union and the company. Several people were injured, including two policemen, and seventeen people were arrested as key participants in the riot. Police and workers battled the rioters. Shots were fired, and police eventually quelled the riot. Bail was set at $100 a piece for the participants. Among those charged were Miss Mary Champlain of Slocum Avenue, a WPA worker; John Zink, a machinist residing on Seymour Street; and Edward J. Manion of Seymour Street.

Fortunately, riots are not a fixture in Syracuse's history. There will continue to be labor disputes, college students will protest or simply act the fool and ethnic bigotry will always be a part of the human condition. As long as these trends continue, there will be a potential for civil unrest and riots in Syracuse.

Chapter 27

MAKING MONEY THE OLD-FASHIONED WAY IV:
MORE FRAUDS AND SCHEMES

I f you've checked your spam folder in your e-mail lately, there is likely at least one message from a purported Nigerian prince or oil minister asking you to help them transfer money for which you'll be handsomely compensated if you will just give them account numbers and a mere pittance of cash in return. Or perhaps you've received a warning e-mail from a government agency asking for help in trapping criminals who are rifling bank accounts. Both scenarios, as most of us are aware, are schemes to rifle your bank accounts. That they still continue in spite of numerous warnings every year is due to the fact that some people will do anything for easy, unearned money. That is as true in the Salt City as it is anywhere else. Shall we look for more bunco artists?

In August 1898, Syracuse police investigated claims that a female bunco artist was operating in the city. Allegedly, the woman, who was in her forties, had approached the congregations of the Universalist, Unitarian and Fourth Presbyterian Churches in Syracuse. Alternately identified as Mrs. Price, Mrs. Rice or Mrs. Gates, she approached members of the congregation or the minister and told them that the mistress of the house in which she was staying sent her to have the minister tend to the mistress. She then asked for a sum of money to return home. Apparently, she had some success with this ploy.

Two years earlier, Syracuse police arrested Josie Russo and Gaetano Petrecca for bribery and robbery. Mrs. Russo claimed to be married to a man charged with bilking Vleto Street of $500 in a bunco game. The bribery charge stemmed from the pair's attempt to "settle the case" by offering Street

The Lincoln County Jail was typical of other nineteenth-century lockups throughout the country. *Courtesy of Peggy Reilly.*

$200. The pair claimed to hail from Newark, New Jersey. Russo had served time in Auburn and Ossining Prisons prior to this arrest.

If ever the phrase *caveat emptor* (Latin for "let the buyer beware") applied, it was when Seward E. Lewis bought a horse-and-buggy from Arthur Reno in December 1904. Lewis claimed that the horse-and-buggy was sold under false pretenses. Reno had allegedly claimed that the horse was sound and gentle, but according to Lewis, the horse was not only blind in one eye but also a kicker. Reno also claimed that the buggy had been manufactured by Moyer. Lewis stated that Moyer did not make the buggy despite the Moyer placard affixed to the carriage. He asked $250 in damages. It was further alleged that Reno knew the horse was blind in one eye when he bought it from Elisha Steadman. Reno denied the charges. He had previously been exonerated in Minoa town court, prompting Lewis to sue in county court. Apparently, the swindle didn't start with used car salesmen.

It's a headline that could grace a Syracuse newspaper today: "Drawing Jury for $185,000 Fraud Suit." Add three or four zeroes to that, and the article almost writes itself. John N. Derschug, the president of the Syracuse Washing Machine Company, stood accused in December 1931 of misrepresenting the company's stock. Edward H. O'Hara, publisher of the *Syracuse Herald*, alleged that Derschug advised him to purchase and hold Syracuse Washing Machine stock while Derschug was, in fact, divesting himself of his shares at inflated prices. Derschug denied any fraud or wrongdoing. O'Hara won his case, but when Derschug appealed, the verdict of the lower court was overturned. The original trial took fourteen days. The case brings new meaning to the phrase "airing one's dirty laundry."

Throughout the early twentieth century, Father Divine generated controversy. The son of slaves, Divine began preaching at an early age and declared himself God. Though he never practiced his particular brand of religion in Syracuse, one of his followers figured in a notable fraud case in the Salt City. In May 1949, the cousins of the late Mary Sheldon Lyon sued Patience Budd. They also named Father Divine and his church in the suit. The root of Miss Budd's legal problems stemmed from Mrs. Lyon's 1943 will, which bequeathed her property to Father Divine. The deceased woman's cousins alleged that Mrs. Lyon drew up another will in 1946 but was prevented from signing it by Miss Budd. Budd had been serving as Mrs. Lyon's secretary and maid when Mrs. Lyon passed away. Judge Zoller ordered Budd to produce all relevant documents and records to support her defense. Mrs. Lyon's relatives petitioned the court to subpoena Father Divine, George Baker and Joe Baker to testify about their knowledge of the 1946 will. Budd argued for a change of venue to New York County, but that motion was denied. The plaintiff's lawyers threatened two witnesses with arrest if they continued to ignore subpoenas to testify. In August 1949, charges of contempt of court against Miss Budd were dismissed when it was determined that she had not received payment to testify as a witness and that the order to present herself to give testimony was delayed. The finding did not include the charges that she used undue influence to keep Mrs. Lyon from signing the alleged new will. On April 19, 1950, the court ruled against Mrs. Lyon's relatives, and the 1943 will was held valid. The court maintained that the cousins did not produce enough evidence to sustain their case. Did Patience Budd coerce Mrs. Lyon into not signing a new will? The allegation is a distinct possibility. It is also possible that Miss Budd and Father Divine were brought to trial because of the reverend's controversial ministry and the fact that they were African American. Sixty-two years later, we may not know the motives of any of the participants, but we can surmise that the trial kept Syracuse readers glued to the pages of their morning papers.

Fraud continues to be a part of life in the twenty-first century. The advent of the Internet makes all of us susceptible to the con man. Joseph Weil was right about one thing—there will always be people who want something for nothing. And as long as there are, the frauds, con games and moneymaking schemes will persist in the Salt City and throughout the world.

Chapter 28

THE WEIRD AND UNUSUAL:
MORE CRIMES OF THE HEART

Poets claim that love is blind. An unknown sage claimed love is stupid. I tend to agree with the anonymous philosopher. We do stupid things when we're in love, and sometimes that gets us in trouble with the law. We're susceptible to the vagaries of our hearts and will continue to be until the big blue marble we call home disappears into the shadowy mists of time.

It was a trend that started with the advent of World War II. The women were called "Allotment Annies." The basic idea was that a woman would marry a GI, who would in turn sign over a portion—if not all—of his pay in an allotment to her. She would milk the guy for all she could and then take a powder. In the movies, these women were portrayed as foreign-born, but the truth is that most were citizens of the United States. Lieutenant Matthew Bahelka of Syracuse sued his wife, Frances, for fraud. The couple married while Bahelka was stationed in Texas and Frances was attending nursing school. The B-17 bombardier was sent overseas when war broke out. While her husband was flying combat missions, Frances sent him a "Dear John" letter explaining that she had married him while on the rebound from a former affair and didn't love him. The former Flying Fortress crewman and prisoner of war was granted an annulment of his marriage on April 11, 1946.

In court with Bahelka was Newton Palmer. Now let's own up guys, we've all stretched the truth a little to impress some young lady, and Mr. Palmer was not immune to a little fibbing. Palmer told his wife, Alverta, that he was forty-seven, he was only married once before and that he had had one child. In reality, he was sixty-nine, this was his fourth trip down the aisle and he had five children. Suffice it to say that Mrs. Palmer wasn't amused when she learned the truth. She sued for annulment on the grounds of fraud and was granted a divorce. If you're going to lie to your spouse, Newton, keep it believable. Really, Mrs. Palmer? I'd get your vision checked.

April 11, 1946, was a busy day for annulments. Donald Leon Douglas was not a man to let a trifle like a felony record keep him from marrying the woman he loved. Of course, it should be mentioned that our would-be Romeo failed to mention his criminal past to his wife, Dorothea. When the couple married in 1944, she had no idea about his lengthy rap sheet. His record came to light when he was arrested for parole violation and remanded to Auburn Prison. Dorothea was awarded an annulment. Not taking the trash out might buy you a night sleeping on the couch, but not telling your wife you're a felon on parole ensures that you'll be sleeping alone when you get out of the pokey.

How do you know your wife is not alive? In 1941, James Campbell was charged with bigamy. Campbell asserted that he believed his first wife, Nellie, whom he had not seen for fourteen years, was dead. He had been living with Hazel Latant and had four children with her. When told they would have to get hitched or their relief would be discontinued, the couple married. The prosecution dismissed the charges on the grounds that James had married in good faith after making several fruitless attempts to locate his first wife. The charges were dropped on the condition that Mr. Campbell immediately start annulment proceedings. It was easier to disappear in the days before computers and DNA.

Perhaps our aforementioned sage was thinking of Harry Nichols when he made the comment above. I'm sure Mr. Nichols had no intention of starting 1928 off with a bigamy charge. Our stalwart was in court to face a charge of non-support brought by his first wife. Being an intellectual giant, he saw no harm in bringing wife number two to court with him. In his defense, he had told his first wife, Sylvia, that he wanted to remarry, and she jokingly told him to go ahead. He had also asked for the engagement ring he gave Sylvia so that he could avoid the expense of buying a second one. He didn't get the ring. The first marriage had ended three weeks after Harry proved to be a little too free with his fists. Sylvia and Harry had a son at the time of his arrest. Apparently, it never occurred to Sylvia or Harry to actually get a divorce. Mae, wife number two, knew nothing of her husband's first marriage. It was reported that she fainted when Nichols introduced wife number one. The non-support charge was supplemented with a bigamy charge, and Harry was held without bail. I wonder if he was the smart one in his family.

It seems that men aren't the only ones to conveniently forget they are married. Sophronia May Beach Neri was arrested for bigamy in 1932 after she attended court for Joseph Neri, who was under indictment for robbing a gas station. During that trial, the bigamy was brought to light, and Sophronia was placed under arrest. The charged alleged that she was still married to Myron Beach, whom she had married in 1928. When questioned by the district attorney, she confessed and was remanded to the county jail to await sentencing. Joseph Neri was acquitted of the robbery charge after Sophronia failed to show up to testify. The state gives you a piece of paper suitable for framing that tells you and everyone else that you're married. Apparently, Sophronia failed to consult it when she married Joseph Neri.

Apparently, lapses in memory were just as common in 1899 as they were in 1928. George Albert Thurston was in court on January 21, 1899, to answer a charge of non-support brought by Lizzie Keller. It came out that in spite of Thurston's lapses in memory, he had at least three wives and was still married to all of them. Thurston denied having any children. Lizzie, Thurston's second wife, dispelled this bout of amnesia. When arrested, George was living with Mary Madison, his third wife, and her father. George apparently didn't pay attention to the Ernest D. Tyler case. Get your scorecard! You can't tell who the players are without a scorecard!

You would think that people would know that having more than one spouse at the same time is illegal in this country, but Ella Thompson Traver Alpeter apparently didn't get that memo. Shortly after World War I, Ella married Arthur Traver, a disabled veteran of the Great War. The couple had two children together, and things appeared fine to Art. In 1926, Ella married Albert Alpeter. According to Alpeter, she told him she was single. She maintained that Alpeter forced her to marry him at gunpoint. Arthur separated from Ella when he discovered her other marriage. Both gentlemen were granted annulments. Mrs. Traver-Alpeter did not appear in court. The bigamy charges started a custody fight for the Travers children between Arthur's mother and Ella's mother. Ella's stationary must have been expensive!

We don't hear a lot about bigamy these days. Along with the improvements in technology, people can now do their own background checks. They may not be doing them, but the Bureau of Vital Statistics does when you apply for a marriage license, so perhaps the days of bigamy are over, save for certain religious sects. Time will tell. And let's face it, if our unknown philosopher is right, people will find a way to use love to get in trouble with the law.

Chapter 29

GETTING HORIZONTAL:
MORE PROSTITUTION IN SYRACUSE

Peple have been getting busy since the dawn of time. There are some who maintain that sex is what makes the world go round, and who knows, maybe they're right. Usually, what happens in the bedroom stays in the bedroom. That doesn't apply if you're paying for sex or, conversely, charging for providing that particular service. Ask ten customers why they purchase the services of a "working girl," and you'll get ten different reasons. Ask ten harlots why they sell themselves, and you'll get an equal number of reasons. In some circles, sex is a commodity. In Syracuse, it is illegal to sell that commodity.

Volney Fowler was arrested on June 19, 1857, by Officer Walsh and charged with keeping a house of prostitution. He was held on bail of $500, and when it was not paid, he became a guest of the county. On the same day, Matilda Davenport, a soiled dove from the village of Palmyra, New York, was sent to the penitentiary for thirty days. Apparently, Officer Walsh didn't appreciate her enterprising nature.

Elisha Mosher and Desdamonia Woodruff were arrested by Syracuse police officers Eckle and Segar on January 5, 1859, and charged with being inmates of a house of prostitution. The women were convicted and sentenced to either pay a ten-dollar fine or spend sixty days in the county prison. It doesn't sound like a happy ending to me.

In June 1865, the Civil War was effectively over, and Syracuse boys were returning home. Harriet Russell was glad to do her part in welcoming them home—for a small monetary consideration, of course. Justice White rewarded her hospitality with a sixty-day stay as a guest of the county. Harriet Steel of Auburn also received sixty days' guest accommodations at the same institution for providing the same services for a stipend.

Five months earlier, on January 21, 1865, Syracuse police raided a bordello run by Hannah Pitcher and Delia Spencer at 104 Madison Street. They were in pursuit of two men wanted for causing a riot. "Romeo" McElhern and Alonzo Spencer fired at Officer Schug. The two men and the women were eventually taken into custody at the bawdy house. The house of ill fame was located not far from the current county courthouse.

We sometimes think of prostitution as a recent phenomenon; however, the practice dates back to the gaslight era. In 1877, Lydia "Spot" Graham was arrested and charged with public prostitution. Her paramour, Robert Mason, was charged with keeping company with a prostitute. The couple was taken into custody on University Avenue. Somebody got an education.

Clara Stevens was arrested on a charge of being a public prostitute on May 3, 1894. Her live-in lover, Thomas Keeler, was simultaneously charged with assault. Both were fined twenty-five dollars. Emma Atkinson was charged

The Weighlock Building in Syracuse at the junction of the Erie and Oswego Canals in 1889. *Courtesy of the Library of Congress.*

A Civil War soldier returns from the war in this 1863 *Harper's Weekly* illustration. Though two years before the end of the war, such scenes were common in 1865, and as troops

returned, the soiled doves were there to "greet" them—for a small fee, of course. *Courtesy of the Library of Congress.*

at the same time with being a public prostitute. She was sentenced to pay twenty-five dollars or serve ninety days in the county prison. Were there private prostitutes in 1894? Ten years later, five Syracuse saloonkeepers and seven women were charged as "disorderly persons." The charge was a euphemism for promoting prostitution. The December 1904 arrests were part of a campaign to curb vice in the city.

Margaret Jane Lambertson was sentenced to six months in Onondaga County Penitentiary after pleading guilty to a charge of vagrant prostitution on July 6, 1950. But your Honor, she was just earning money the old-fashioned way!

Perhaps we hear more about prostitution these days. The newspapers print the names of customers busted in sting operations. The police continue operations against the world's oldest profession, and the practitioners change their location. It is a cat-and-mouse game that will continue in the Salt City and everywhere else.

Chapter 30

SMUT HAPPENS:
OBSCENITY CASES IN SYRACUSE

If you want to start a raging argument, give someone your definition of pornography. Since the advent of the sexual revolution, pornography has been fairly accessible to those who have a taste for it. There are those who think of pornography as a modern phenomenon, but in point of fact, smut was part and parcel of civilization even before Pompeii was covered by lava. Woman's advocate and birth control pioneer Margaret Sanger was charged with sending obscene material through the mail. The material in question was literature advising women on birth-control methods. Church and civic leaders have waged war against pornography throughout the Salt City's history and will continue to given constitutional strictures for the foreseeable future.

Clarence Hill was arrested in 1937 for sending obscene material through the mail. The Onondaga Nation citizen was arraigned in federal court and pleaded not guilty to the charge. Hill allegedly sent a fourteen-year-old girl an obscene letter. The girl's mother turned over the missive to federal authorities. Hill was jailed in the Cedar Street jail when he could not furnish the $2,000 required for bail.

Henry Frankel was convicted on June 25, 1937, of selling obscene literature to high school students in the city. Frankel pleaded guilty and was awarded thirty days in the county pen.

On May 10, 1937, Raymond J. McHale, a twenty-eight-year-old WPA worker, was taken into custody after police raided an impromptu theater on Wolf Street for showing an indecent movie. The offense was McHale's

Margaret Sanger, a leading advocate for women's rights, was arrested for advising women on methods of birth control under the government's obscenity laws of the time. *Courtesy of the Library of Congress.*

second and earned the federal employee a stern rebuke from Judge Homer Walsh after he pleaded guilty. McHale paid a fifty-dollar fine and was given a thirty-day suspended sentence. Walsh warned the convict that he would go to the penitentiary if he were seen in court again. Police also charged Patrick Onerio with promoting the blue film. Frank Kowicki, the owner of the building in which the stag film was shown, was not charged, as there was no evidence that he knew the nature of the entertainment before he rented the hall to McHale. Three reels of film were seized during the raid. Two hundred spectators eluded capture by police in the raid. I thought the feds paid good wages.

A book on vintage combat aircraft nose art sits on my bookshelf. As a historian, it gives me insight into the minds of the young men who flew and fought in World War II, Korea and Vietnam. But back in 1949, the seller of this book might have faced charges of violating obscenity laws! On February 19, 1949, Syracuse police arrested Emmanuel Slutzker after he sold a twenty-one-year-old man three obscene cartoon books. Police confiscated a number of cartoon booklets and photos of nude women in Slutzker's possession. The youth had been questioned by police, who saw the cartoon books in his possession and had him return with a marked bill to buy more of Mr. Slutzker's wares. Slutzker was fined $750 and ordered to cooperate with police if any more purveyors of pornography should approach him. Six years later, Hugh Hefner would launch *Playboy* magazine, and society would change forever.

A few months later, Syracuse police, aided by the FBI, arrested meat salesman Simon Gordon for sending obscene materials through the mail. The charge was brought after police arrested Joseph Lostumbo for selling pornographic comic books in his North Salina Street snack bar. Lostumbo identified Gordon as the smut purveyor. Lostumbo cooperated after he was brought in front of Justice Bamerick. The judge was reported to be irate over the number of obscenity cases coming in front of him and was determined to make an example of the snack bar owner if he did not assist authorities in bringing the supplier to heel. Vice squad detectives arrested Gordon after talking with Lostumbo and obtaining a search warrant. The feds assisted and pursued a charge of interstate transportation of obscene materials, a federal offense at the time. Stick to cold cuts the next time, guys!

In 1950, six people were arrested for selling obscene pictures. Two brothers were the last arrested on February 24, 1950. Albert and Felix Restuccia of Seymour Street were charged with developing the risqué photos after Marcus Adams, also of Seymour Street, was convicted of selling the photographs. Three other people were scheduled to appear in court in connection with the case. They were charged with being the subjects of the dirty pictures. I guess Fibber Magee and Molly weren't on the radio.

Ten years earlier, Bernard T. Groginski pleaded not guilty to a charge of disorderly conduct. Though the specification dealt with Bernard allegedly throwing a rock at a girl's house after she failed to keep an appointment with him, obscenity was involved. Groginski threatened to break every window in the girl's house if she did not meet with him. When the girl's father answered the door with a flashlight in hand, Groginski threw a rock at the house. Police focused on the rock throwing, but when confronted by the police, the suspect also confessed to making obscene phone calls to over one hundred women and sending obscene letters to some of them over a two-year period. Police held Groginski on the charges in lieu of $1,000 bail. Your dating techniques seriously need work, Bernard.

I doubt Miss Manners would approve of Leo Castleman's conduct—the police certainly didn't. Castleman was arrested on July 20, 1948, for using obscene language on the phone. Police trapped Castleman after making obscene phone calls to a girl who, with the assistance of a friend, was able to keep him on the phone until police could arrest him. He was held in lieu of $500 bail. I guess Castleman missed the lecture on phone etiquette.

On August 5, 1920, Jesse E. King was fined $300 for sending obscene letters to his former fiancée, Miss Amy Slocum. Apparently, King didn't take their break up with equanimity. He was also given a suspended sentence of

In 1915, operators still dispatched calls. With the advent of direct dialing, placing a call became easier, and obscene callers could hide in anonymity. *Courtesy of the Library of Congress.*

a year in the crossbars hotel. Jesse should have consulted Miss Manners for post-breakup conduct advice.

We don't hear much about pornography these days unless it deals with the exploitation of children. Several cases over the past sixty-two years have asserted that the first amendment covers speech that might be considered morally reprehensible. Obscene phone calls usually come under the anti-stalking laws that most communities have in place. It isn't hard to find pornography in Syracuse even if you don't have a computer, and unless it deals with kids, you won't get tossed in the clink for it.

Chapter 31

SPEAK SOFTLY AND CARRY A BIG STICK: THE ROOSEVELT/BARNES TRIAL

Theodore Roosevelt is one of those people that you either love or hate. President Roosevelt did great things in his life, but he wasn't afraid of stepping on toes to do so. Politics was part and parcel of "TR," and he could brawl with the best of them. Roosevelt was a controversial man, even within the Republican Party. Never a wallflower, Roosevelt spoke his mind and let the pieces fall where they may.

The trial that would grip Syracuse for over a month and keep newspapers selling like hotcakes started after Colonel Roosevelt compared William Barnes to his democratic counterpart, Charles Murphy, calling them both political bosses. In those last days before World War I, accusing a politician of "bossism" was akin to calling him a thief and a liar on a grand scale. Roosevelt made his statement on July 22, 1914, and it was carried in most major newspapers in the country.

William Barnes Jr. wasn't surprised by the former president's allegations. Rumors of political corruption and cronyism followed him throughout his political career. The publisher of the *Albany Times Union*, Barnes was the grandson of political mover and shaker Thurlow Weed. Barnes was heavily involved in both national and New York politics, and he promptly sued Roosevelt for libel.

The two combatants arrived in Syracuse on April 18, 1915. President Roosevelt emerged from the Southwestern Limited with a smile but referred all questions about the trial to his counsel, John Bowers. During the trial, he stayed with local politico Horace Wilkinson. Barnes arrived on the same train with his retinue of aides and his counsel. Unlike Roosevelt, the crowd did not recognize him. Barnes's attorney denied that the trial was about politics. Neither man entertained the idea of settling out of court.

William Barnes was seeking $50,000 in damages. The trial was held in Syracuse after Roosevelt's lawyer successfully argued that the former president could not get a fair trial in Albany County. Both sides dug into the political past of the other, and Roosevelt expected the trial to last at least two months. He also told his son Kermit that he would rather go to jail than retract anything he said about Barnes. It was expected that the court would call over one hundred witnesses.

Despite Attorney Ivins's assertion that the trial was not political, both men would be affected by the outcome. If Barnes won, the Progressive Party would be destroyed and Roosevelt eliminated as a political threat in New York. Ironically, Roosevelt's victory in the trial assured the same thing. He maintained that he was not against the Republican Party but elements that hindered progress and honest government. The presiding judge, Justice Andrews, was a Harvard classmate of Roosevelt's, but that former association held no sway with Andrews. Roosevelt commented to his son Kermit that Andrews was fair but narrowly "legalistic"[26] in his rulings.

President Theodore Roosevelt was sued by William Barnes. The case was tried in Syracuse. *Courtesy of the Library of Congress.*

Both Barnes and Roosevelt testified during the five-week trial. Roosevelt spent nine days testifying, while Barnes was on the stand for four days. Though Roosevelt believed at the outset that his vindication would return him to an active political life,

William A. Barnes Jr. was a mover and shaker in New York State and Republican political circles. His suit against Teddy Roosevelt kept newsboys busy. *Courtesy of the Library of Congress.*

The fourth Onondaga County Courthouse, where the Roosevelt/Barnes trial was held in 1915. The Beaux Arts–style building still serves the county's judicial needs. *Courtesy of Neil K. MacMillan.*

such was not the case. By the end of the trial, he confided to his son Kermit that he would not return to public life. Though Roosevelt won, he estimated the trial cost him between $30,000 and $40,000. Barnes and his attorney did not stay to hear the verdict, according to Roosevelt, who did stay.

Both men were surprised by the outcome of the trial. Barnes saw Roosevelt's statements as libelous and believed that the jury would uphold his case. Though Roosevelt knew he was popular with the crowd, he believed the trial would go against him due to the fact that the judge had ruled out most of his evidence. President Roosevelt died on January 6, 1919. Barnes lived another eleven years, passing away in July 1930. Both men were fighters who relished combat for its own sake and both would have rather gone down in flames than admit they were wrong. Perhaps the final assessment for the trial is that they were too much alike to compromise. The trial packed hotels in Syracuse and entertained readers across the country. It was a newsman's dream, and it kept the current county courthouse packed for the duration of the trial. For Syracuse, it was the trial of the century.

Chapter 32

SYRACUSE AND CRIME:

A COMPARISON OF THEN AND NOW

Welcome back to the twenty-first century, but let's not close the door just yet. As we look back, we find that the crimes we think are unique to our time really aren't. Technology has improved both the commission and the detection of crime, and several landmark cases leveled the playing ground to ensure that all received a fair trial.

Syracuse also evolved. From a sleepy crossroads named Bogardus Corners, the Salt City grew to a thriving metropolis, in large part because of the salt industry and the Erie Canal. With the growth came the crime that follows every population center. Syracuse's growth even prompted some to campaign to have the Salt City made the state capitol. I have to wonder how much crime that would have generated.

Some of the crimes I've mentioned bring more questions than answers, and as we've learned, that is all too frequently the case. Not everyone mentioned was found guilty. In news reports across all media, we see and hear the word "alleged" when crimes or wrongdoings are discussed. The word is used to avoid lawsuits such as the one brought against Theodore Roosevelt discussed in the previous chapter. You'll find it in here, as well, for the same reason.

Let's face it—crime is history. Why did Edmund Hillary climb Mount Everest? "Because it was there," he claimed. We find similar reasoning when it comes to criminal endeavors. As I stated above, criminals suffer from the same foibles that the rest of us do. People do stupid things. If they didn't, movies like *Jackass* and television shows like *America's Funniest Home Videos*

Various styles of manacles and handcuffs. *Courtesy of Peggy Reilly.*

would tank before they ever got to the production phase. We do things for the hell of it. To understand why criminals do things is to understand why the rest of us do them.

A riot is what led to Syracuse becoming a city. The Salt City would have become a city without the riot, but perhaps a bit differently and a bit later. The riot had to happen. Syracuse grew and continues to grow and change. Each crime mentioned in this missive changed the city, if only on a tiny scale. The famous and not-so-famous stood in the dock to have their day in court. Some were run to ground here. Charles Dickens visited Syracuse in 1870 shortly before he died. He was unimpressed, calling the Syracuse House the worst hotel he'd ever stayed in. Dutch Schultz had a more favorable impression, even while in police custody. Obviously, I lean towards Schultz's assessment.

Anytime you look at crime, you come away with questions. I have several that may never be answered. Frank Matty never gained the mayor's office; that job went to his rival, James K. McGuire. What would Syracuse's future have been with Matty at the helm? Matty reminds me of Chicago's William "Big Bill" Thomson, who asserted in the 1920s that "Chicago ain't ready for reform." I can hear that sentiment coming from Matty. Political patronage continued well after the spate of political trials in the late 1890s and the

Roosevelt-Barnes trial. A Syracuse mayor would go to prison for political corruption almost a century after the Candee and Matty trials. Ironically, he is remembered for bringing jobs to the Salt City.

While we didn't have a Jesse James or a Butch Cassidy in Syracuse, we did have Oliver Curtis Perry. Bold and brash, with a bit of education, Perry could have succeeded in almost anything he put his hand to. I find that many of the men and women who populate these pages had the same drive that characterized Perry. Some chose a less confrontational method of purloining their ill-gotten gains, and they told a good story even if it wasn't believable. You probably won't see the con men on the streets these days. The advent of the computer and the Internet has opened new vistas for the grifter just as it did for the counterfeiter. Joseph Weil would marvel at it, but he might be a bit disappointed, too. After all, if any dope with a keyboard can run a scam, where's the challenge?

The tawdry-made way stops in the Salt City. If Ruth Snyder wasn't physically in Syracuse, her troubled spirit was with Judd Gray. The passionate love affair became the proverbial "he said she said" round of accusations. Judd was visiting friends in Syracuse when he was captured. Mr. Snyder might have lived a long life if Henry Judd Gray had grown a spine and simply told Ruth, "No." Snyder might have killed him alone, but Syracuse would not have been linked to what Damon Runyon called the "Dumbbell Murderers."

The canal and the salt industry gave Syracuse vitality. Although men like William Blake were rough

Even in 1879, there were laws prohibiting making your own whiskey. Many judges and juries turned a blind eye to the problem during Prohibition. *Courtesy of the Library of Congress.*

hewn, they did help build the Salt City, and perhaps it is fitting that Syracuse was graced with that moniker. I stated above that we need the examples of men like Ephraim Webster and Asa Danforth, and I stand by that. But Syracuse also needed men like Oliver Curtis Perry, Benjamin Roscoe and Hiram Davis. We learn little if we do not have the not-so-perfect to study. Smirk all you want, but remember that none of us are terribly far from the peccadilloes I write about here.

If Chicago wasn't ready for reform in the 1920s, Syracuse wasn't ready to give up booze. Bootlegging was a way to avoid what was seen as unwarranted government intrusion into personal matters. Like suffrage, Prohibition was a divisive issue. Bootlegging still goes on, only these days it's in the form of CDs and DVDs. We don't see a lot of it here in Syracuse. These days, the culprits hide in foreign countries. Still, the government doesn't want you selling homemade hooch.[27] But raise a glass or two to those who sidestepped the law. They might not have been the brightest bulbs in the pack, but they sure gave us a chuckle or two.

The sun is coming up. Yes, Bank Alley is still dark, but the streets will be busy soon. We should go, but can you hear the ghosts of the Salt City's crime history? The chap with the luxuriant moustache is Mr. Matty. Give him a wave. James Harvey still walks his beat along Water Street, at least on the pages of history books. Give Oliver a nod; he has a train to catch. If you're in the courthouse and hear raised voices, it's just the Colonel and Mr. Barnes. I'll leave you here. The miscreants are slumbering for now.

EPILOGUE

I hope you enjoyed my guided tour of Syracuse. Though I have lived all over, the Salt City will always be my home. We often fail to look at the darker side of our history, and to my thinking, that is akin to trying to read a book with half the pages missing. There are more tales of mayhem out there, and perhaps you'll let me share them with you. Each day we live, we make history. I hope to share more of the Salt City's history with you. Until then, best wishes!

NOTES

1. It is unknown what sort of weapon Charles Seigle used, as both pistols and long guns were generally smoothbore at this time.
2. A demijohn is a bottle, usually covered in wicker basketwork on its lower third portion, holding between one and ten gallons.
3. It is not known exactly what Crandall's device looked like. I went by descriptions of the devices found in articles from the *Syracuse Courier* held by the Onondaga Historical Association.
4. There is no truth to the myth that the term "hooker" derives from Major General Joe Hooker of Civil War fame. The term derives, in fact, from the Corlear's Hook district of New York City. A "soiled dove" is a term from the period for prostitutes. The term "sporting house" is a Gilded Age nicety for a bordello. Horizontal refreshment is an 1860s euphemism for a sex act.
5. Ms. Empie's first name is spelled as it was in the July 25, 1850 issue of the *Onondaga Standard*.
6. Alderman Candee's name has been alternately spelled Candoe in various newspaper accounts.
7. Gray as quoted in "Night After Murder Played With Children at Home of Friends," *Syracuse Herald*, March 22, 1927.
8. Though not included because of the time period this book covers, Officer Wallie Howard Jr. was shot and killed on October 30, 1990, and was the fourth Syracuse policeman murdered on the job.

9. Ironically, the Bureau of Internal Revenue released figures showing that sixty thousand prescriptions were legally issued for liquor in Syracuse in 1922, amounting to one for every third person in the city.

10. The Genna family of Chicago was notorious for making poisonous booze. They were allied with Al Capone until they tried to oust him. Al was not amused.

11. The spelling of marijuana as it was mentioned in the Tax Act of 1937.

12. The same article lists his first name as Connie in one paragraph and Lonnie in another.

13. Bank robbery became a federal crime in the 1930s.

14. *Syracuse Daily Standard*, March 17, 1887. The quote is attributed to Lawyer Kennedy.

15. "Double eagles" were twenty-dollar gold coins, so called because the ten-dollar coin was called an "eagle."

16. The fourth chapter of Genesis details the story of Cain and Abel.

17. These are Burns's words as found in the March 22, 1878 issue of the *Syracuse Standard*.

18. Daily's name is variously spelled as Dally and Daley.

19. These are Gough's words taken from his statement to Paducah, Kentucky police.

20. In those days, the German Section was located on the near north side of the city near Assumption Church on North Salina Street.

21. Bogardus Corners was the original name for Syracuse. It was renamed Corinth, but the postmaster general ordered the town be renamed, as there was already a Corinth, New York. Thus, Syracuse was named.

22. A con man by the name of James Addison Reavis forged papers he claimed were deeds to the Peralta land grants of the 1500s in the American southwest. The supposed Peralta never existed.

23. Halloween is the Christianized version of the ancient Celtic holiday of Samhain, and many of Halloween's customs derive from that old holiday.

24. These are the alderman's words as quoted in the *Syracuse Evening Herald*.

25. The Confederate government actually instituted a draft in 1862.

26. "Legalistic" is Roosevelt's term as quoted from a letter to his son Kermit on May 2, 1915.

27. The law allows a private citizen to make up to two hundred gallons for private consumption.

ABOUT THE AUTHOR

Neil MacMillan was born and lives in Syracuse. He is a U.S. Navy veteran of the Gulf War and holds a BA with disciplines in creative writing and history from SUNY Empire State College. He has worked in a variety of fields. He is a historical re-enactor of the American Civil War. In addition to writing several historical articles about the Syracuse area, he recently finished his debut novel, *There I'll Be a Soldier*. Neil can be reached at nmacmillan@twcny.rr.com.